BIRD GROUPS BY CO

Grebes, albatrosses, petrels, shea
tropicbirds, frigatebirds, cormo
and pelican.

Herons, bitterns, egrets, hamerkop, ibises, spoonbill,
storks, flamingos and ducks.

Eagles, hawks, buzzard, harrier, kites, falcons, francolin,
partridge, quails, guineafowl, rails, mesites, button-quail,
flufftails, crake, gallinules, moorhen and coot.

Painted snipe, snipe, jacana, pratincole, ruff, turnstone,
stilt, crab plover, plovers, godwits, whimbrel, curlew,
greenshank, sandpipers, sandplovers, sanderling, stint,
skuas, gulls, terns and noddies.

Sandgrouse, doves, pigeons, lovebird, parrots, parakeets,
coucal, cuckoos, couas, owls and nightjars.

Swifts, swiftlets, martins, swallow, kingfishers, bee-eaters,
rollers, cuckoo-rollers, ground-rollers, asities, bulbuls,
greenbuls, oxylabes, babbler, thrush, robins and hoopoe.

Rock-thrushes, stonechats, wheatear, wagtails, pipits,
flycatchers, newtonias, cisticola, lark, warblers, emutails,
jeries, white-eyes and sunbirds.

Vangas, tylas, cuckoo shrikes, starlings, drongos, crows,
fodies, sparrows, weavers, canaries, mannikins, finches,
avadavat and waxbill.

QUICK REFERENCE

The number associated with each picture refers to the page
on which the family or genus first appears.

Birds *of the*
INDIAN OCEAN ISLANDS

IAN SINCLAIR AND
OLIVIER LANGRAND

Illustrated by

Norman Arlott ▪ Hilary Burn ▪ Peter Hayman ▪ Ian Lewington

STRUIK

To the memory of Richard K. Brooke, our friend and birding colleague.
Ian Sinclair; Olivier Langrand

Struik Publishers (Pty) Ltd
(A member of The Struik Publishing Group)
Cornelis Struik House
80 McKenzie Street
Cape Town 8001
Reg. No. 54/00965/07

First published in 1998

Illustrations by
Norman Arlott (cover; spine; pages 101–105, 121–123, 127, 149–173)
Hilary Burn (title page; pages 47–59, 107–111)
Peter Hayman (pages 33–45, 61–97)
Ian Lewington (back cover; pages 99, 113–119, 125, 129–147)

Project manager: Pippa Parker
Editor: Peter Joyce
Designer: Dominic Robson
Cover design: Dominic Robson
Maps: Desireé Oosterberg
Proofreader: Jenny Barrett

Reproduction by Hirt & Carter (Pty) Ltd, Cape Town
Printed and bound by Kyodo (Pte) Ltd, Singapore

ISBN 1 86872 035 7

CHAMBERLAIN

Established 1903

SPONSOR'S FOREWORD

Why would a builders' merchant choose to promote and sponsor a field guide to the birds of Africa's island neighbours? Principally because there wasn't one on the shelves, and the gap needed to be filled.

Bird-watching took root as a serious and popular pastime in southern Africa only after the publication of quality, user-friendly field guides in the 1980s. Since then millions of people, both residents and visitors, have enjoyed these books and the world they illuminate.

Birds offer an easy way to become acquainted with, and interested in, the environment: they are found everywhere, they fly around and make a lot of noise, and they are almost infinite in the variety of their shapes and sizes, their colours, habits and habitats.

But one needs access to all of this, something that brings order to the kaleidoscopic diversity of images. Vague interest can then mature into exciting participation, from which concern can develop for the many wonderful but potentially threatened species and the habitats that support them.

The islands on the western side of the Indian Ocean are a treasure trove of beautiful (and sometimes bizarre) animals and plants. This book will help provide the necessary access to one of the most precious components of the region's natural heritage.

DAVID CHAMBERLAIN
Managing Director

Authors' Acknowledgments

Many people have assisted us, both technically and logistically, over years of field work on and around the islands of the region. Our thanks to all, and especially to Jaqui (at Ampijoroa); Lorraine Betts; Tanya and James Brown; David and Margot Chamberlain; Lindsay Chon Seng; Steven M. Goodman; Dominique Halleux; Sheila M. O'Connor; Georges Randrianasolo; Lucienne Wilmé; Ian Davidson; Tony and Maureen Dixon; Nadia Ekhart; Rudi van der Elst; the late Sandra Fisher; Allan Foggit (of Starlight); Dennis Jordan; Sue and Ron Johns; Howard Jolliffe; Michael Lambarth; Lyn Mair; Lorraine and Alf Mauf; the brothers Maurice and Patrice (at Périnet); Erica and John Platter; Loret 'Hypsipetes' Rasabo; Ily Rasmussen; Nivo Ravelojaona; Derek Schuurman; Rob Leslie; Rona and Roy Siegfried; Jackie Sinclair; Adrian Skerrett; Don Turner; Barbara and Giles Webb; and Sandy De Witt. Thanks also to Robert Prys-Jones and his staff at the British Museum.

To our friends at Struik Publishers, who produced this book, go our sincere thanks for their patience, good humour, enthusiasm and encouragement. We are especially indebted to Pippa Parker and Peter Joyce; to Dominic Robson for his fresh and refreshing approach to design, and to Desireé Oosterberg for her meticulous work on the maps.

This field guide involved prolonged periods away from home, and endless hours hunched over the computer, and we thank our families – Jackie and Lucienne, and our children Daryn, Kiera, Sarah and Marion for their support and understanding.

Finally, we are greatly indebted to the sponsors, Chamberlain & Co, who made this book possible. Their sustained interest in the work of authors and artists alike and, especially, David Chamberlain's sense of wonder when immersed in the world of birds, spurred us on both in the field and at our desks.

Artists' Acknowledgments

The four contributing artists express their sincere appreciation to the management and staff of the Natural History Museum, Tring, United Kingdom, for their help in locating reference material. Special thanks are extended to Dr Robert Prys-Jones (NA and PH) and Michael Walter (NA) of the Museum; to Simon Harrap (IL) and to Rob House (PH).

CONTENTS

REGIONAL MAP   10

INTRODUCTION   11

FAMILY INTRODUCTIONS   13

LOCATING ENDEMIC BIRDS

    MADAGASCAR   22

    COMORO ISLANDS   26

    MAURITIUS   28

    RÉUNION   29

    RODRIGUES   30

    CENTRAL SEYCHELLES   30

    ALDABRA ISLANDS   31

SPECIES ACCOUNTS   32

VAGRANTS TO THE REGION   174

GLOSSARY OF TERMS   175

ILLUSTRATED GLOSSARY   176

FURTHER READING   178

INDEXES

    SCIENTIFIC NAMES   179

    ENGLISH COMMON NAMES   182

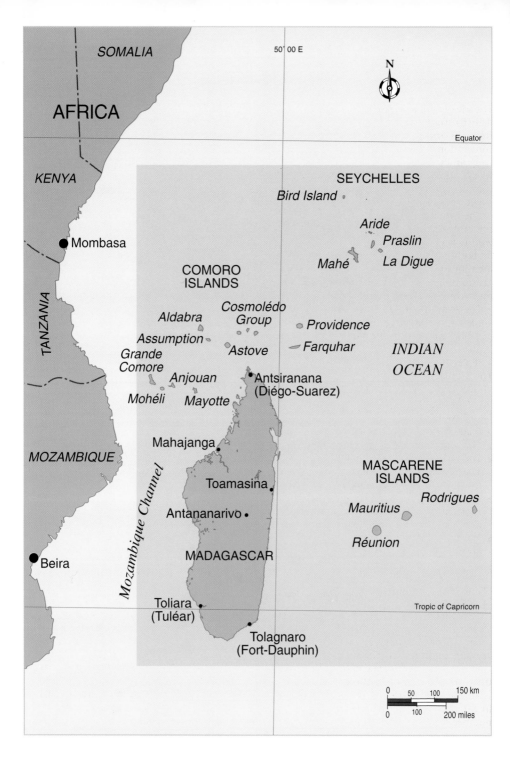

INTRODUCTION

The idea for this book had its first stirrings in the field, on Madagascar, in November 1981. The daily frustrations we encountered in trying to identify many of the island's birds, using what was then the only available literature on the subject (Milon *et al*), were such that we craved a conventional field guide. Part of the problem was solved with the publication, in 1990, of Olivier Langrand's *Birds of Madagascar*, but what we still needed was information on all those species found on the magical islands of the Comoros and Mascarenes. To encapsulate the full avian complement of this extensive region, together with that of the Seychelles archipelago, within a single volume was a project often discussed and now, finally, complete.

The intention of this book is to enable an observer to identify, either quickly or at leisure, all the birds that are encountered regularly within the area. Illustrations, executed by some of the world's leading bird artists, show the various plumage details – pertaining to either age-class or sex or both – and also the in-flight and unusual shape postures where these are important to identification. The text is brief, concise, highlighting recognition characters, preferred habitats, distribution, current status, and vocalization. Each species entry is accompanied by a distribution map which indicates the bird's range within the region or the island to which it is restricted.

The section entitled Locating Endemic Birds (p. 22) is not designed as a general bird-finding guide but, rather, as an island-by-island survey listing specific localities and the birds – species peculiar or unique to the region – that occur in them.

THE REGION DEFINED

The area covered by this book is rectangular in shape, extending lengthwise from latitude 29°S, off the southern tip of Madagascar, north towards the equator. Its eastern limit is longitude 67°E, off Rodrigues in the Mascarene Islands; its western 42°50′ E, which runs between Madagascar and the African coast. Within the region are:

■ Madagascar and its immediately adjacent islands.
■ The Mascarenes, among which are Réunion, Mauritius and Rodrigues.
■ The Comoro Islands, which embrace Grande Comore, Mohéli, Anjouan and Mayotte.
■ The Seychelles archipelago's central (granitic) islands, including Mahé, Praslin, La Digue, Cousin, Cousine, Aride and Frégate.
■ The outlying Aldabras, comprising Aldabra, Astove, Assumption and Cosmolédo. The Amirante banks and the Farquhar and Providence group hold very few land-bird populations, although they are important areas for breeding tropical seabirds.
■ The surrounding western Indian Ocean and the waters of the Mozambique Channel within the given coordinates are also covered, though the ocean distribution of all seabirds is poorly known.

All those species that breed or are thought to breed within this area (generally referred to as 'the region'), together with the migrants and some of the vagrants found here, are covered by the book. Excluded are those species that have been recorded fewer than ten times and are presently thought to be accidental visitors to the region. Migrants and vagrants that occur regularly – annually or almost so – appear in these pages as there is a reasonable chance that an observer will encounter them. Those that have been recorded fewer than ten times in the region appear in the list of vagrants on page 174. The latter are all admirably described in many, and very good, extant field guides, and to have included them in this rather specialized volume would have tended to clutter the plates, diverting attention away from the more important and less well-known endemics.

We have taken the most recent observations, reported in scientific publications, into consideration in establishing the complement of the region's breeding, migrant and vagrant species. The number of these publications, and the amount of detailed information they impart, reflect the growing interest among ornithologists in the various islands of the south-west Indian Ocean.

BIRD NAMES

For the most part we have followed Langrand (1990) in the usage of both common and scientific names throughout the book, deviating only to incorporate recent taxonomic decisions and common-name changes (Clements 1994, Dowsett & Forbes-Watson 1993, and Sinclair *et al* 1997). We also considered the new classification of the world's birds, based on molecular research (Sibley & Monroe 1990, Sibley & Ahlquist 1990), but we decided that the presently accepted arrangement was more suitable for the purposes of a field guide.

SPECIES COVERAGE

Of the 359 fully covered species, the Amber Mountain Rock Thrush *Monticola erythronotus* has recently been defined as a full species using genetic research techniques. The Red-shouldered Vanga *Calicalicus rufocarpalis* has been accepted as a full species from field observations and on morphological grounds. We have not followed the trend towards creating phylogenetic species, but we do treat as full species some of the birds that were previously thought to be subspecies – decisions based on comparative field studies over a long period. Planned genetic research will go a long way towards confirming the full species status of the following:

- Madagascar Sacred Ibis *Threskiornis bernieri*. Confined to western Madagascar and the Aldabra islands. Distinctive in having a pale blue eye, and in flight shows no black tips to the primaries and secondaries.
- Aldabra Rail *Dryolimnas aldabranus*. Confined to and isolated on several islands on the Aldabra atoll. The bird is wholly terrestrial, and is smaller than the White-throated Rail *D. cuvieri* of Madagascar. Its plumage also shows some subtle differences.
- Comoro Green Pigeon *Treron griveaudi*. Isolated on Mohéli in the Comoros. Generally smaller and greyer with yellower underparts than the Madagascar Green Pigeon *T. australis*, and its call sequence is higher pitched and more rapid.
- Olive-capped Coua *Coua olivaceiceps*. Occurs alongside Red-capped Coua *C. ruficeps* in the forests of western Madagascar, and replaces it in the south-west. The two species do not inter-breed. Apart from the obvious plumage differences, the Olive-capped Coua's call is higher in pitch and rather more prolonged.
- Madagascar Black Swift *Apus balstoni*. Confined to Madagascar, and possibly also found on the Comoro Islands. In the field, it is very different from the African Black Swift *A. barbatus*: generally paler, with a more extensive white throat, and very scaly on the underparts. The birds observed on Grande Comore and Anjouan resemble Madagascar Black Swift.
- Comoro Cuckoo-Roller *Leptosomus gracilis* from Grande Comore. Very much smaller than Madagascar Cuckoo-Roller *L. discolor*, showing clear plumage differences and with a higher-pitched, more rapid call sequence. Cuckoo-rollers on the remaining three islands of the Comoros do not greatly differ from the Madagascar Cuckoo-Roller.
- Madagascar Hoopoe *Upupa marginata*. Very much larger than African and Eurasian hoopoes *U. africana* and *U. epops*, and with a very different call and song.
- Kirk's White-eye *Zosterops kirki*. Has a much brighter-yellow plumage than any other of the region's white-eyes, and shows a very broad white eye-ring.
- Mayotte White-eye *Z. mayottensis*. Has obvious chestnut flanks. The white-eyes on the island of Mohéli are very similar to Madagascar White-eye *Z. maderaspatanus*.
- Mauritius Grey White-eye *Z. mauritianus*. The flanks are much less orangey, and the upperparts greyer, than Réunion Grey White-eye *Z. borbonicus*, and the bill is longer and more decurved.
- Comoro Green Sunbird *Nectarinia moebii*. Confined to Grande Comore; larger than Madagascar Green Sunbird *N. notata*, with a purple (not blue or green) iridescence to head and breast. The female is paler on the underparts, with much less streaking.
- Abbott's Sunbird *N. abbotti*. Confined to Cosmolédo, Astove and Assumption islands in the Aldabra group. Similar in size to Souimanga Sunbird *N. souimanga*, but has a deeper-red

breast-band, and black belly and vent. The bird is very similar to Anjouan Sunbird *N. comorensis* but has yellow (not vivid orangey-red) pectoral tufts.

- Comoro Blue Vanga *Cyanolanius comorensis*. Larger than Madagascar Blue Vanga *C. madagascarinus*, and its upperparts are a different shade of blue – more lilac, and more uniform, lacking the contrast between crown and mantle. Juvenile is a more uniform rusty-buff on the underparts.
- Comoro Cuckoo Shrike *Coracina cucullata*. Smaller than Madagascar Cuckoo Shrike *C. cinerea*, with white (not grey) underparts. There is also an olive morph (lacking in the Madagascar Cuckoo Shrike).
- Aldabra Red Fody *Foudia aldabrana*. A strikingly coloured fody, its plumage much more vivid than that of Forest Fody *F. omissa*. It is a generally larger bird; shows a bright-yellow belly, which contrasts with the red breast, and has a chunkier bill.

FAMILY INTRODUCTIONS

GREBES   Podicipedidae   page 32
Small, aquatic (mainly freshwater) diving birds with lobed (not webbed) feet. They show a distinct head-pattern in breeding plumage; young have striped head-patterns and seek refuge on parent's back. Gregarious outside breeding season. Three species occur in region, of which two are endemic. The Alaotra Little Grebe is now thought to be extinct.

ALBATROSSES   Diomedeidae   page 34
Very large, long-winged seabirds which are largely confined to the southern oceans. They feed mostly on squid taken at the surface, and are dynamic gliders, often travelling long distances by using favourable, strong winds. Three species occur in the region as vagrants and three on a more regular basis, mostly during the austral winter.

SHEARWATERS AND PETRELS   Procellariidae   page 36
Variable, ranging from small, pigeon-sized petrels to giant petrels. True seabirds, coming ashore only to breed; all have tubenoses, a feature they share with the albatrosses. Thirteen species occur in the region, two of which are endemic and four are vagrants.

STORM PETRELS   Oceanitidae   page 40
Tiny seabirds which share the tubenose feature of the larger petrels and albatrosses. Very swallow- or swift-like in appearance, hugging the ocean's surface, sometimes appearing to dance over the water on pattering feet. Four species occur in the region, all of them vagrants.

TROPICBIRDS   Phaethontidae   page 42
Snowy-white seabirds typified by their long central tail feathers, which are either red or white. Fast, pigeon-like flight, often high above the ocean surface. The birds plunge-dive to obtain their food, and rest for long periods on the ocean surface. Two species occur in the region.

PELICANS Pelecanidae page 44
Very large birds with distinctive, long bills which have an extended pouch used for scooping fish. They swim with the head held low, lunging forward to catch prey. All four toes are joined by webs. Dynamic soarers, riding thermals with ease. One species occurs in the region, but has not been seen for many years.

BOOBIES Sulidae page 44
Large, white or brown seabirds with deep-based, long, pointed bills. They are plunge-divers, often descending from a considerable height, sometimes swooping after flying fish. Three species occur in region.

CORMORANTS AND DARTERS
Phalacrocoracidae and Anhingidae page 44
Long-necked and long-tailed waterbirds with variable black and white plumage; four toes webbed. They swim low in the water, rising from surface with small dolphin-like leap. They grab or spear fish prey; sit for long periods drying or warming themselves with wings outstretched. Two cormorants and one darter occur in region. One of the cormorants is a vagrant.

FRIGATEBIRDS Fregatidae page 42
Distinctively long-winged black seabirds with long, forked tails. Shape angular. Very aerial, rarely landing except to breed and never on water. Pirate boobies, terns and tropicbirds to rob them of food. Two species occur in the region.

HERONS, EGRETS AND BITTERNS Ardeidae page 46
Sizes vary. Mostly aquatic birds which feed principally on fish, amphibians and insects, which they catch mainly by wading in water. White members of the family are usually referred to as egrets; larger members are called herons. Bitterns are shy, skulking birds, with cryptic coloration. A total of 19 species occur in region, one of which is endemic and another a breeding endemic.

HAMERKOP Scopidae page 52
Distinctive feature of this bird is an unusually shaped crest and flattened black bill, which combine to create the hammer-shaped head. Long legs designed for wading; bill adapted for gripping amphibians. Very raptor-like in flight; builds enormous nests. One species occurs in the region.

STORKS Ciconiidae page 54
Large, long-winged, short-tailed birds with long bills. Lumbering in flight but dynamic thermal gliders. They usually frequent wetland. One species has an unusual space between the mandibles. Three species occur in the region, one of them as a vagrant.

IBISES AND SPOONBILLS   Threskiornithidae   page 52
Medium-sized birds with long, decurved or flattened bills. They frequent forests or wetlands, and feed by probing or, like spoonbills, with a side-to-side sweeping motion. Variable white and brown plumages, some with ornate crests. Four species occur in the region, one of which is endemic.

FLAMINGOES   Phoenicopteridae   page 54
Very long-legged, long-necked, pink birds with sieved, bulbous bills used in filter feeding. Two species occur in the region.

DUCKS   Anatidae   page 56
A family of aquatic birds, highly varied in size and coloration, whose members spend much of their time swimming on open water. Occur in large flocks or singly; form 'V' formations in flight. Well-known 'quack' vocals from many species, of which 14 occur in the region, three of which are endemic. One, the Madagascar Pochard, might be extinct.

ACCIPITERS   Accipitridae   page 60
This family comprises a diverse range of predatory birds. Groups relevant to the region are listed below.

Eagles Medium-sized to large birds of prey, which are both fish- and meat-eaters. Feathered legs are characteristic. Noted for their soaring flight and hunting talents. Four species occur in the region; two are endemic, two extreme vagrants.

Buzzards Generally smaller than eagles, and lack the latters' feathered legs. Most have piercing, mewing calls. Known for the diversity of their plumage, which varies from juv. through to ad.; many variables in full ad. plumage. One endemic species occurs in the region.

Goshawks and sparrowhawks Small to medium-sized birds with short, rounded wings and long tails. Goshawks are normally larger than sparrowhawks; all have bright-yellow or orange eyes and legs. Some characterized by very long toes and nails, enabling to grip feathered prey. Three endemic species occur in the region.

Harriers Long- and thin-winged birds with unusual flight action, the wings held in shallow 'V' as they hunt, flying close to and quartering the ground. They have partially flattened facial discs (as in owls) and very long, thin legs. Two species occur in the region, one endemic, the other a vagrant.

FALCONS   Falconidae   page 64
Dynamic hunting birds, with long, pointed wings and slender bodies. Some perform high-speed aerial strikes at prey. Ten species occur in the region, four of which are endemic.

FRANCOLINS AND QUAILS   Phasianidae   page 68
Small, plump-bodied terrestrial birds with variable cryptic
coloration, many with diagnostic crowing and call notes.
Usually found in pairs or small groups; flight straight and
rapid on whirring wings. Five species occur in the region, one
of them endemic, one introduced.

GUINEAFOWL   Numididae   page 68
Medium-sized, rotund, terrestrial game birds with white
speckled plumage and horny casque on head. Domesticated
in many places. One introduced species occurs in region.

MESITES   Mesitornithidae   page 70
Terrestrial rail-like birds with short, rounded wings and long
tails, which they constantly flick. They are capable of flying,
but hardly ever do so. They are inevitably seen walking slowly
along the forest floor. Found in small groups or pairs; highly
vocal. The family, whose taxonomic origin is mysterious, is
endemic to the region, and comprises three species.

BUTTON-QUAILS   Turnicidae   page 70
Very small, terrestrial, quail-like, cryptically coloured birds of
woodland and grasslands. Unusual in their role-reversal, the
male being duller and undertaking parental care. One
endemic species occurs in the region.

RAILS, CRAKES, FLUFFTAILS, GALLINULES,
MOORHENS AND COOTS   Rallidae   page 70
Mainly small, wetland- and forest-dwelling birds, most of them
very furtive. Most have short tails, which are constantly flicked;
many are good swimmers. Sixteen species occur in the region,
seven of which are endemic.

JACANAS   Jacanidae   page 76
Aquatic birds with very long toes and nails, which enable
them to walk on floating vegetation. Most play reverse sexual
roles, the male undertaking full parental care. Sociable and
noisy, sometimes gathering in flocks. One endemic species
occurs in the region.

PAINTED SNIPES   Rostratulidae   page 76
Plump-bodied shorebirds with long bills, short rounded wings
and short tails. They frequent freshwater and brackish wetlands. A polyandrous species, the male undertaking all
parental duties. One species occurs in the region.

STILTS AND AVOCETS   Recurvirostridae   page 78
Stilts and avocets are delicate, long-legged shorebirds with
bills that are either straight and thin (stilts) or thin and
upturned (avocets). Plumage mostly pied black and white;
toes partially webbed (avocets). Avocet is vagrant to region.

CRAB PLOVER   Dromadidae   page 78
Black and white shorebird with long legs and a unique, thick-based, short, black bill used in dismembering crabs. Highly social and sometimes found in large groups. The only shorebird that nests in underground burrows. One species, a migrant, occurs in the region.

PLOVERS   Charadriidae   page 78
Shorebirds varying in size from small to medium, with short bills and long legs. They are found in a wide variety of habitats ranging from wetlands to deserts. They feed with a deliberate walk-stop-and-peck action. Twelve species occur in the region, including one endemic and one vagrant.

SNIPES, GODWITS, SANDPIPERS, STINTS, CURLEWS
         Scolopacidae   page 76
This diverse group ranges from tiny, sparrow-sized stints to chicken-sized curlews, with a variety of shapes and bill types. Apart from Madagascar Snipe, all the region's such birds are summer migrants and vagrants from the northern hemisphere, where they breed. Twenty-seven species occur, 15 of which are vagrants and one an endemic.

PRATINCOLES   Glareolidae   page 76
Unusual short-legged birds with very long wings and deeply forked tails. They are crepuscular, feeding on insects taken on the wing. Flight action reminiscent of that of a large swallow. Four species occur in the region, one as a breeding endemic, the other three as vagrants.

SKUAS, GULLS AND TERNS
         Stercorariidae and Laridae   page 88
Small to large waterbirds, both oceanic and inland. Very variable; colours range from black through brown and pink to white; feeding behaviour extends to extremes of parasitism (skuas). Terns are normally smaller than gulls and have forked tails. Twenty-five species occur, of which 12 breed in the region and one is vagrant.

SANDGROUSE   Pteroclidae   page 98
Medium-sized, short-legged, cryptically coloured gamebirds with feathered legs and toes. Flight is pigeon-like; habitat semi-arid, long distances covered in quest of drinking water. One species, an endemic, occurs in the region.

PIGEONS AND DOVES   Columbidae   page 98
The smaller members of this extensive family are usually referred to as doves, the larger ones as pigeons. They are unusual in the copious amounts of powder down they have in their plumage, in the 'pigeon milk' they feed their young, and in their ability to drink direct (by suction) rather than

with scoops of the bill. Fifteen species occur in the region, of which seven are endemic and five introduced.

PARROTS AND LOVEBIRDS Psittacidae page 104
Small to medium-sized birds with plumage ranging from bright-green to drab. Bills are heavily hooked, short and stubby, powerful, designed for cracking open nuts. Flight can be either rapid and direct or slow and languid. Six species occur in the region, of which five are endemic and one introduced.

CUCKOOS, COUAS AND COUCALS Cuculidae page 106
All the birds in this family are characterized by a reversible fourth toe; most have long tails. Cuckoos do not build nests but, rather, lay their eggs in the nest of a host, who then raises the cuckoo young. Couas and coucals, on the other hand, build nests and raise their own young. Couas have short wings, long tails and brightly coloured, fleshy areas around their eyes. Coucals have powerful bills, a slow, awkward flight action and, on the ground, clamber clumsily through vegetation in search of insects. Seventeen species occur in the region, of which 10 are endemic, one is a breeding endemic and four are vagrants.

OWLS Tytonidae and Strigidae page 112
Nocturnal, predatory birds with talons comprising two toes that point forward and two backward. Vocalization covers a wide variety of hoots, shrieks and whistles. They are silent fliers, with specially structured soft feathers. Plumage is often heavily barred or streaked. Eleven species occur in the region, of which seven are endemic and two are vagrant.

NIGHTJARS Caprimulgidae page 114
Nocturnal birds with very large mouths, with which they catch insects on the wing. Heads and eyes are unusually large, legs very short and weak. Super-cryptic coloration provides highly effective camouflage. Two endemic and one vagrant species occur in the region.

SWIFTS Apodidae page 116
These non-perching birds are airborne most of the time, their long, thin, scythe-shaped wings enabling effortless flight. Larger species are among the world's fastest-flying birds. Eleven species occur, of which four are endemic and three vagrant.

KINGFISHERS Alcedinidae page 120
Small fish- and insect-eating birds, many with dazzling blues and orange coloration. They have long, dagger-shaped bills and very short legs, with two toes pointing forward and two backward. The posture is upright. Birds either plunge-dive for fish or hunt for insects in the forest. Two endemic species occur in the region.

BEE-EATERS   Meropidae   page 120

Typically, members of this family have greenish or blue plumage, thin bodies, pointed tails and long, thin wings. Their bills are long, thin and decurved. The birds hawk insects from exposed perches, are usually gregarious, and are buoyant and swift in flight. Two species occur in the region, one of which is a vagrant.

ROLLERS   Coraciidae   page 122

Their display flights give these birds their common name: they tumble and 'roll' over and over in the air uttering raucous calls. They are large-headed and stout-billed, with purplish or blue coloration. Rollers feed largely on insects taken on the wing and are partly crepuscular. Two species occur in the region, one as a vagrant.

GROUND-ROLLERS   Brachypteraciidae   page 124

Unusual, large-headed, stout-billed terrestrial birds found in rain forest and subarid thorn scrub. Their plumage is soft and loose, the colour range including bright blues and reds and cryptic camouflage patterns. The birds, which dig nesting tunnels, are very secretive and elusive. The family is endemic to Madagascar and comprises five species.

CUCKOO-ROLLERS   Leptosomatidae   page 122

Large-headed and stout-billed birds with soft, loose plumage. Very marked sexual dimorphism. Species typified by its peculiar flapping, gliding and rolling display flight, which is accompanied by repetitive whistling calls. The family, which consists of two species, is endemic to the region.

HOOPOE   Upupidae   page 132

Typical features of this family include a long, erectile crest, long decurved bill, pinkish body, and black and white barred wings and tail. The birds are terrestrial feeders; flight action is undulating. Strong smell serves as predator deterrent. One endemic species occurs in the region.

ASITIES   Eurylaimidae   page 126

Forest (rain and dry) birds typified by the brightly coloured wattles over their eyes. Bodies are rotund, tails short. The two larger species are fruit-eaters; the two smaller ones, which feed on insects and nectar, have long, decurved bills. Four endemic species occur in the region. The four formerly constituted an endemic family (Philepittidae), which is now an endemic subfamily within the Eurylaimidae.

LARKS   Alaudidae   page 140

Small, terrestrial birds, usually with brown or earthy-coloured plumage and a generally drab appearance. They are known for their diverse and melodic vocalization, often involving mimicry and uttered while in flight. All are ground-nesting. One endemic and one vagrant species occur in the region.

SWALLOWS AND MARTINS — Hirundinidae — page 118

Very swift-like in appearance, though totally unrelated to swifts. The birds are very aerial, hawking their insect prey on the wing, but regularly perch on wires and twigs. They build domed or cupped nests, from mud pellets, or excavate tunnels in sandbanks. Six species occur in the region, one of which is an endemic breeder and two are vagrants.

CUCKOO SHRIKES — Campephagidae — page 162

Unobtrusive, rather sluggish forest birds, whose females vaguely resemble cuckoos. Mostly grey or grey and white with rufous and olive plumages. Primarily insectivorous, they glean insects in an unhurried fashion through the canopy. Four endemic species occur in the region.

DRONGOS — Dicruridae — page 164

Mostly black, upright-postured, perching birds with forked tails and stout bills. Aggressive towards large raptors and crows, giving aerial chases. Calls loud and grating, with mimicry a prominent element. They display flycatcher-like feeding behaviour in forests or open terrain. Four species, all endemic, occur in the region.

CROWS — Corvidae — page 164

Large black and white or black and grey birds with thick, stout bills and raucous, croaking calls. The black plumage shows iridescent blues and purples. Highly adaptable, found in all areas and especially near human habitation. Two species occur in the region, one of them a recent arrival.

BABBLERS, OXYLABES, GREENBULS AND JERIES — Timaliidae — page 130

An unusual mixture of terrestrial and arboreal birds whose affinities are not clear: few characteristics are common to the family as a whole. A strictly forest-dwelling family, social, frequently occurring in small groups. They are also prominent in mixed-species groups observed feeding within the forest. Most forage on the ground, creeping about in the under-growth. Only a few have clearly defined songs and calls. Twelve species occur in the region, all of which are endemic.

BULBULS — Pycnonotidae — page 128

Small to medium-sized arboreal birds which, in this region, are dark-plumaged with dark caps and pink bills that vary in size. For the most part noisy and conspicuous, frequenting different types of woodland, feeding on fruits and insects. Six species occur in the region, of which five are endemic and one introduced.

THRUSHES AND CHATS   Turdidae   page 132
Small forest-dwelling (thrushes) and open-terrain (chats) birds. Chats have an upright posture with tail and wings flicking; thrushes bound along the forest floor, and scratch in leaf litter. Highly vocal with melodic songs. Thirteen species occur in the region, of which seven are endemic and four vagrant.

WARBLERS, CISTICOLAS, EMUTAILS AND NEWTONIAS
                                Sylviidae   page 140
A wide variety of small, insect-eating birds, all with drab olive or brown plumage, most with diagnostic calls and songs. Habitats range from scrub to reed-beds and forest to thicket. Twenty-six species occur in the region, of which 22 are endemics and four are vagrants.

FLYCATCHERS   Muscicapidae and Monarchidae   page 138
Small, sometimes very long-tailed birds which move in hyperactive fashion through wooded habitat. They have an upright, perching posture, and dash after insects, which they glean or catch in flight. Calls are subdued, but some utter rich trills. Six species occur in the region, of which four are endemic.

WAGTAILS AND PIPITS   Motacillidae   page 136
Terrestrial birds, either brightly coloured, yellow, grey and black (wagtails) or drab brown and streaked (pipits). Wagtails have very long tails, pipits shorter ones, but both constantly wag them up and down (wagtails more frequently). Six species occur in the region, one of which is an endemic and two are vagrants.

VANGAS   Vangidae   page 156
Small to medium-sized birds with basic pied and chestnut-coloured plumage. Forest-dwelling. The wide range of bill shapes reflects specific evolutionary adaptations. Sixteen species in family, which is endemic to region.

STARLINGS   Sturnidae   page 162
Stocky, robust birds with short, pointed bills and thick, strong legs. Forest-dwelling and open-country species; flight powerful and direct. Four species occur in the region, one endemic, one introduced and two vagrant.

SUNBIRDS   Nectariniidae   page 152
Small, brilliantly coloured birds that feed chiefly on nectar and have long, decurved bills for probing flowerheads. They also feed on insects. Females have drab, non-iridescent plumage. Eight species occur in the region, all of which are endemic.

WHITE-EYES   Zosteropidae   page 148
Small, warbler-like birds with white eye-rings and plumage which is a drab mix of green, olive and yellow. They pierce

flower-bases for nectar and have an unusual 'brush'-tipped tongue. They also feed on insects and fruit. Nine species occur in the region, all of which are endemic.

SPARROWS, WEAVERS AND FODIES   Ploceidae   page 170
Small, compact birds with short, conical bills. Some build elaborately woven nests in colonies. Most are grain-eating and form large flocks, especially when roosting. Eleven species occur in the region, nine of which are endemic and two introduced.

WAXBILLS, MANNIKINS AND CANARIES
                Estrildidae and Fringillidae   page 172
Small, seed-eating birds which are terrestrial in habits, but use trees and scrub for nesting. Most have drab, dun-coloured plumage. Canaries, though, are usually bright yellow (and highly vocal). Many species are kept as cage-birds. Eight species occur in the region, one of which is endemic, the other seven introduced.

LOCATING ENDEMIC BIRDS

Visiting birders to the islands covered in this book will of course be especially interested in those species that are unique to a particular island or area. This chapter is designed to serve as a general guide to locating the many endemic birds (but not the more common residents and migrants), and to the conditions on the ground – accommodation, travel facilities and so on – that one can expect to find in the various places.

MADAGASCAR
Madagascar has been isolated from the African landmass for some 165 million years, and as a result most of its plants and animals have evolved in isolation, which has produced a remarkable variety and a high level of endemism among species. The island's birds have been subject to similar evolutionary imperatives, though the diversity is not as great as that of other such large tropical islands as Borneo, Java and Papua-New Guinea, mainly because there are no islands between the African mainland and Madagascar, and thus no stepping stones for colonization. Madagascar is also too far away from Asia for that continent to have been a significant source of colonization.

More than half of Madagascar's breeding birds are endemics that are found nowhere else on Earth, so the island is an essential destination for those who want to learn about the world's bird life in its entirety.

Because Madagascar is a large (and still developing) country, you should plan on investing quite a bit of time in search of the full complement of endemics. Most can be found and observed if you spend, say, three weeks visiting five separate areas. Generally, the best way of getting around is by air (only two sites are easily and rapidly accessible by road from the capital, Antananarivo). Domestic flights are reliable, and they serve the island's main centres. There are hotels close to the major birding spots, but their capacity is fairly limited so it is advisable to book well in advance.

Just how good the birding is will be affected, to some extent, by the season. In the rain forest, for instance, the birds – and especially the ground-rollers – are silent and tend to be inactive during the dry cold season (May–August). Winter viewing in the deciduous dry forest and the subarid thorn scrub, on the other hand, is generally good.

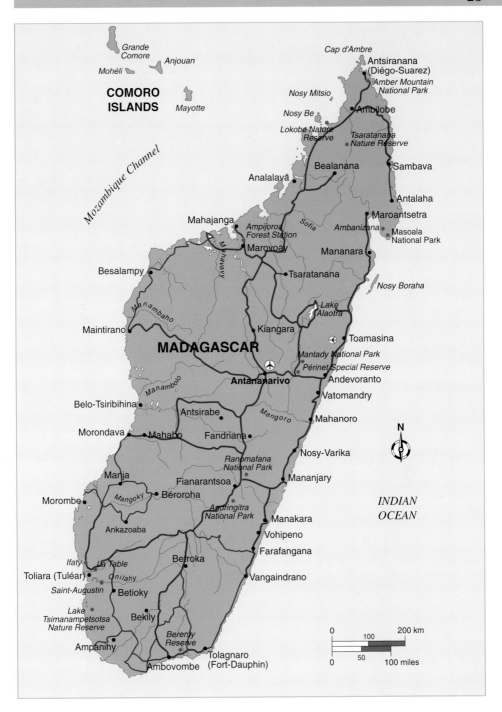

Grande
Comore
Anjouan
Mohéli
Mayotte

**COMORO
ISLANDS**

Cap d'Ambre
Antsiranana
(Diégo-Suarez)
Amber Mountain
National Park
Nosy Mitsio
Nosy Be
Ambilobe
Lokobe Nature
Reserve
Tsaratanana
Nature Reserve

Mozambique Channel

Bealanana
Sambava
Analalava
Antalaha
Maroantsetra
Mahajanga
Ampijoroa
Forest Station
Ambanizana
Masoala
National Park
Marovoay
Sofia
Mananara
Besalampy
Tsaratanana
Nosy Boraha

Mahavavy

Manambaho

Maintirano
Kiangara
Toamasina
Lake
Alaotra

MADAGASCAR
Mantady National Park
Périnet Special Reserve
Andevoranto
Antananarivo
Vatomandry

Manambolo

Belo-Tsiribihina
Antsirabe
Mangoro
Mahanoro
Morondava
Mahabo
Fandriana
Nosy-Varika
Ranomafana
National Park
Manja
Fianarantsoa
Mananjary
Béroroha
Mangoky
Morombe
Andringitra
National Park
Manakara
Ankazoaba
Vohipeno
Farafangana
Ifaty
La Table
Betroka
Toliara (Tuléar)
Onilahy
Vangaindrano
Saint-Augustin
Betioky
Lake
Tsimanampetsotsa
Nature Reserve
Bekily
Ampanihy
Bereny
Reserve
Tolagnaro
(Fort-Dauphin)
Ambovombe

N

INDIAN
OCEAN

0   100   200 km
0   50   100 miles

Périnet (Analamazaotra)

Périnet, also known as Analamazaotra, is three hours' drive (six by train) east of Antananarivo, and is the most popular of Madagascar's birding spots: a mid-altitude forest site, it has more than 110 species on its list, including many endemics. They can be seen along a network of fairly well maintained trails. Some of the local guides, who can be hired on the spot, are highly skilled and speak English. There is also good birding along the road to the fish-ponds, on the hill above the ponds, and on the main trail that starts at Green Lake and runs a few kilometres to end at the summit of a ridge (the route passes through numerous forest micro-ecosystems). Périnet is classified as a Special Reserve, and you'll need a permit to enter, which can be obtained at the entrance gate or, in advance, from the Association Nationale pour la Gestion des Aires Protégées (ANGAP), BP 1424 Antananarivo (101), Madagascar. There are several hotels near the reserve.

Madagascar Little Grebes breed on Green Lake and are visible throughout the year; the Madagascar Squacco Heron can be seen on the fish-ponds and lake; the Cryptic Warbler and Short-legged and Pitta-like ground-rollers along the main trail; the elusive Dusky Greenbul and the Red-breasted Coua are observed regularly on the hill above the ponds (this is probably the only easily accessible place hosting these two species). Périnet is also an excellent spot for some widespread endemics such as Madagascar Crested Ibis, Blue Coua, Velvet Asity, Sunbird-Asity, Wedge-tailed Jery, Nuthatch Vanga, and Tylas.

Mantady

Located a few kilometres north of Périnet lies Mantady National Park, which holds some rare species not found in Périnet. Access is now much easier than it was – thanks to the recently opened Vakona Lodge – but its network of trails is still being developed, so the going can be a bit rough. However, Mantady is well worth visiting as its recent observations have revealed some of the rarest endemics, among them the Brown Mesite, Red-breasted Coua, Red Owl, Scaly Ground-Roller and Helmet Vanga. Permits should be obtained in advance from ANGAP (see Périnet above).

Ranomafana

Ranomafana National Park, proclaimed to protect the mid-altitude rain forest, is located about 10 hours' drive from Antananarivo and two hours' from Fianarantsoa. There is basic accommodation in the small village of Ranomafana. Permits are obtainable either at the entrance gate or from ANGAP in Antananarivo (see Périnet above). Ranomafana offers probably the most skilled of the island's nature guides. The park has an excellent trail network; there's also very good birding along the main tarmac road linking Vohiparara with Ranomafana.

Ranomafana is *the* place for ground-rollers. The Pitta-like Ground-Roller is common; Rufous-headed and Short-legged ground-rollers can be located if you put in some work; the Grey-headed Greenbul, Brown Emutail, Yellow-browed Oxylabes, Forest Rock-Thrush and Pollen's Vanga are easily found. Recent observations have also revealed Madagascar Serpent Eagle and Yellow-bellied Sunbird-Asity. The forest marshes are home to the elusive Madagascar Snipe and Grey Emutail.

Berenty

The privately owned Berenty Reserve lies some two hours' drive west of Tolagnaro (Fort-Dauphin). Excellent accommodation is available right in the middle of the gallery forest running along the Mandrare River. The nearby subarid thorn scrub holds some species restricted to this type of habitat, among them Running Coua and Subdesert Brush-Warbler. Despite the reserve's small size it has a well-planned network of trails, and it is a good place to observe the Madagascar Sparrow-hawk, Giant Coua, White-browed Owl and Madagascar Scops Owl. Humblot's Heron is fairly common on the Mandrare River. Night walks in the gallery forest and subarid thorn scrub will usually provide excellent sightings of White-browed Owl and Madagascar Scops Owl. Around 100 bird species have been observed in this protected area, which attracts more visitors than any of Madagascar's other reserves.

Ifaty

About 28 km north of Toliara (Tuléar) lies a large block of subarid thorn scrub where some of Madagascar's unique bird species can be seen. This is the only place, for instance, where the two monospecific genera, both belonging to two endemic families, are in residence. The Subdesert Mesite and the Long-tailed Ground-Roller are common near the Ifaty area's resort hotels. Local villagers, who work from the nearby hotels, are expert at locating these two species. You are also likely to see Banded Kestrel, Running Coua, Thamnornis Warbler, Archbold's Newtonia, Sickle-billed Vanga, and Subdesert Brush Warbler. The grassy stretches around the area's seasonal ponds are home to Madagascar Plover. A number of places in Ifaty and Toliara offer accommodation. No permits are required to visit the area.

Saint-Augustin; La Table

If you are in the Toliara region, a day-trip to Saint-Augustin, 30 km to the south, will enable you to see an additional three localized endemics: Verreaux's Coua, found in the subarid thorn scrub of the hills surrounding Saint-Augustin, and the Subdesert Rock-Thrush of the coastal dune-bush. Saint-Augustin is accessible by road; on the way, make a point of stopping at the flat-topped hill known as La Table, where the newly discovered Red-shouldered Vanga can be found, together with species restricted to subarid thornscrub, such as the Subdesert Brush Warbler. No permits are needed.

Ampijoroa

The Ampijoroa Forest Station, next to the highly controlled Ankarafantsika Strict Nature Reserve, is easily reached after a three-hour drive from Mahajanga (Majunga). There are no hotel facilities, so visitors will either have to make a day-visit or camp out. Be prepared for an early start to the day: this is one of the island's most rewarding birding spots. As well as the deciduous dry forest, you'll see some very interesting wetland species at and near the Amboromalandy dam, about 30 km west of Ampijoroa along the main road. Humblot's Heron and Madagascar Jacana are fairly common; Bernier's Teal is regularly seen. The necessary permit to visit Ampijoroa can be obtained from the Direction des Eaux et Forêts, BP 243 Antananarivo (101). Local guides will help you find your way around the excellent network of trails. Two of these lead through the most humid part of the forest (Botanical Garden Trails A and B), where you can see White-breasted Mesite and Schlegel's Asity; others take you through the driest areas of the so-called Sandy Plateau, also home to White-breasted Mesite and to the very localized Van Dam's Vanga. Highly visible endemics around Ampijoroa include Coquerel's and Red-capped Couas, Madagascar Pygmy Kingfisher, and Rufous Vanga. Ravelobe Lake, near the Ampijoroa Forest Station, hosts a pair of Madagascar Fish-Eagles, a threatened species.

Amber Mountain

The Amber Mountain National Park, located 25 km south of Antisranana (Diégo-Suarez), hosts some interesting rain-forest birds. You will need an entry permit (available from the regional office of ANGAP in Antsiranana, or at the park entrance). Road access is usually trouble-free but can be difficult on rainy days, when the steepness of the slopes turns driving into something of an adventure. The park has an excellent trail network and you won't need a guide. This is a rewarding area for Madagascar Crested Ibis, Pitta-like Ground-Roller, Dark Newtonia, and White-throated Oxylabes, but its special drawcard is the local endemic, the Amber Mountain Rock-Thrush. The bird can be found both on the route leading to Grande Cascade and along the Botanical Garden Trail.

Small lakes in the forest may reveal the Madagascar Little Grebe and Madagascar Squacco Heron. The park merits either a one- or two-day trip. Accommodation is available in Antsiranana.

Masoala

The Masoala National Park, which lies in the north-east, protects the largest tract of rain forest left on Madagascar, and it serves as sanctuary for some very interesting bird species. Access, however, is rather difficult. The easiest way to get there is to fly to Maroantsetra (though buying the air ticket can be a laborious process), and then take a boat to the western coast of the Masoala Peninsula to reach the village of Ambanizana. From there, narrow trails lead through the forest, which is home to that most remarkable of vanga species, the Helmet Vanga. Here, too, you will see Red-breasted Coua, Scaly Ground-Roller, Bernier's Vanga and the recently (and regularly) observed Madagascar Serpent Eagle and Madagascar Red Owl, two rare endemics that hold special interest. The necessary permit to visit the park can be obtained in Maroantsetra. The park's management team might be able to provide you with a local guide to take you through the forest. Masoala is well worth more than a day's visit, so you will either have to put up in one of the very basic shelters or camp out. Be prepared for long walks on steep and often slippery terrain.

COMORO ISLANDS

GRANDE COMORE (NGAZIDJA);
MOHÉLI (MWALI); ANJOUAN
(NDZUANI); MAYOTTE (MAORE).

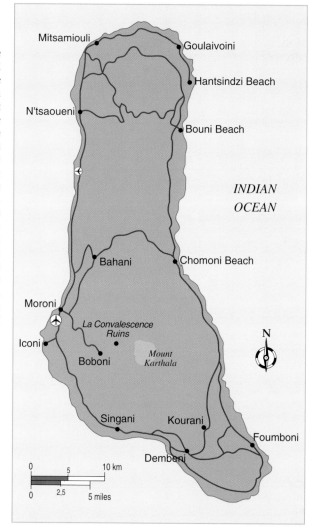

The four components of the Comoro group are the least visited of the region's islands and are therefore rather less well known to ornithologists than are most of the others. Getting to Grande Comore and birding on this, the largest island of the group, is relatively easy; finding your way to the remaining three can be problematic unless you take the very basic inter-island ferry, a charter flight, or one of the irregular inter-island flights. Car-hire facilities are available, and *taxi brousse* (a rudimentary bush taxi) will get you around the others. All four of the islands offer at least basic accommodation, and Grande Comore and Mayotte provide a fairly wide choice of places to stay.

Grande Comore

Endemic birds: Comoro Pigeon; Karthala Scops Owl; Comoro Cuckoo-Roller; Comoro Drongo; Comoro Thrush; Comoro Bulbul; Humblot's Flycatcher; Comoro Cuckoo Shrike; Kirk's White-eye; Karthala White-eye; Comoro Brush Warbler; Humblot's Flycatcher; Comoro Green Sunbird; Comoro Fody.

All of these birds can be found on Mt. Karthala, which has the largest crater of any of the world's active volcanoes. An overnight stop on its upper slopes will be necessary if you want to locate the Karthala Scops Owl and Karthala White-eye.

Arrange beforehand, at the village of Boboni, for a guide and (if you intend overnighting) a porter to take you through the forests to the heathland near the summit. Starting at first light, follow them along the well-beaten track near Boboni and work the forests uphill. All the listed endemics except Karthala White-eye can be seen in the forest, and, except for the Comoro Drongo, all are relatively easy to find. Make camp at the ruins on the open grassland area known as La Convalescence. The owl is common in forests near the campsite. In the morning, proceed to the summit and search for the white-eye in the stunted forests and heathland. Assuming you find the bird fairly quickly, you can comfortably make the return journey to Boboni the same day. It is also possible to approach the volcano's crater from the village of Kourani, but there are no good camping sites along the way. On the other hand, you are more likely to find the Comoro Drongo, which is the least common of Grande Comore's endemic species, on this route.

Mohéli

Endemic birds: Comoro Blue Vanga; Benson's Brush Warbler; Comoro Green Pigeon.
On foot from Fomboni, the main centre on the island, take any track or trail leading to the island's distinctive forested ridge. Best route is east of the village of Fomboni and just beyond the river. Follow the higher path each time the track forks. The endemics are common and easy to locate.

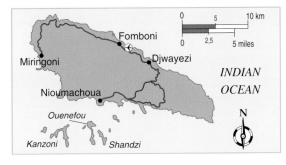

Anjouan

Endemic birds: Anjouan Scops Owl; Anjouan Sunbird.
The Anjouan Sunbird is common and seen just about everywhere. The owl, however, is more elusive, and your search will involve either camping out or a long night walk. Take a taxi from Mutsamudu to Dindi, near Tsimbeo (make a point of telling the driver you want to be taken to Dindi and not Dzindi, which is the larger of the two villages). The very steep, forested slopes above Dindi and the area around Lake Dzialandze are the most promising, though it will still be difficult to locate the owl unless you bring a tape to solicit response. Ask for a local guide, one who knows both the area and the bird (which is known locally as the Bandanga), and be prepared to overnight on site.

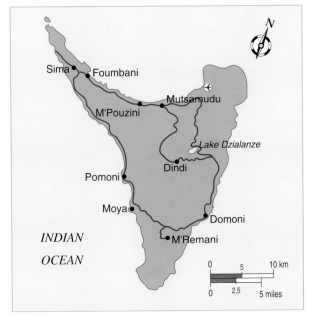

Mayotte

Endemic birds: *Mayotte Drongo; Mayotte White-eye; Mayotte Sunbird.*

From Mamoudzou, the main centre, take a *taxi brousse* to Pic Combani, the nearest stretch of montane forest. Continue on to the end of the road and walk the last 1–3 slightly sloping kilometres. All three endemics are easily located along this track and in the adjacent woodland.

Watching the sea from headlands and from the inter-island ferry might produce Wedge-tailed and Audubon's shearwaters, White-tailed and Red-tailed tropicbirds, Greater and Lesser frigatebirds, Brown, Red-footed and Masked boobies, the Lesser Noddy, and Bridled, Sooty, Greater Crested, Common, and Black-naped terns.

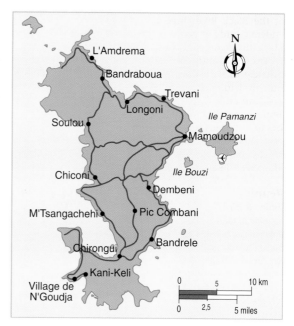

MASCARENE ISLANDS

MAURITIUS; RÉUNION; RODRIGUES.

Two of the three islands, Mauritius and Réunion, are easily reached by regular international flights. Flights connect daily between Mauritius and Réunion but only three times a week from Mauritius to Rodrigues. A broad range of accommodation is available on the two main islands. Mauritius has car-hire facilities and plenty of taxis, and guides (at Black River) who are knowledgeable about their island's bird life. Rodrigues has one hotel, and a *taxi brousse* will take you to the few remaining forest patches.

Mauritius

Endemic birds: *Mauritius Kestrel; Pink Pigeon; Mauritius Parakeet; Mauritius Cuckoo Shrike; Mauritius Bulbul; Mauritius Olive White-eye; Mauritius Grey White-eye; Mauritius Fody.*

To locate and observe all the Mauritian endemic birds means time spent in the Black River Gorges National Park and, specifically, in the Macchabé-Bel Ombre Nature Reserve (the only endemic species seen outside the reserve is the Mauritius Grey White-

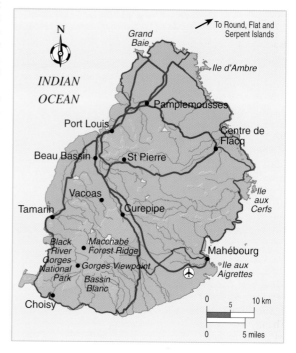

eye, which is common throughout the island). Contact the Mauritian Wildlife Appeal Fund's staff, at the Black River Breeding Centre, for a guide who will virtually guarantee finding all the endemic birds. If you want to go it alone, on the other hand, visit Alexander Falls, Bassin Blanc, Black River Gorges Lookout and the Macchabé Forest Ridge. All these areas are well marked on the tourist maps, and offer both easy and pleasant bird-watching.

A trip to Round Island, preferably in the afternoon, will reveal a good selection of seabirds, notably Trinidade Petrel (or Round Island Petrel to those who admit the latter as a full species). A boat can be chartered from Grand Baie in the north-west of the island; a tour taking in Round, Serpent and Flat islands should involve 3–5 hours' sailing time. Aim to be offshore at Round Island 1–2 hours before sunset to coincide with the arrival of the petrels; look for them high above the island's peak. Other seabirds to be seen on the trip include Wedge-tailed, Audubon's and Mascarene shearwaters, Red-tailed and White-tailed tropicbirds, Greater and Lesser frigatebirds, Masked and Red-footed boobies, Lesser Noddy, Sooty, Bridled, Roseate and Common Noddy terns.

Réunion

Endemic birds: Réunion Stonechat; Réunion Black Petrel; Barau's Petrel; Réunion Cuckoo Shrike; Réunion Bulbul; Réunion Olive White-eye; Réunion Grey White-eye.

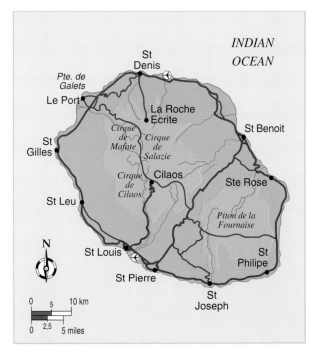

From Saint-Denis, the island's capital, drive to La Roche Ecrite, which is the beginning of a well-used and well-marked hiking trail. It is preferable to start out at first light because the later morning and early afternoon is often either rainy or misty. Follow the trail for 3–5 km and you should see all the passerine endemics. The most elusive, the Réunion Cuckoo Shrike, is best sought in forest close to the trail in the vicinity of a tall fence with a convoluted gate (this is at the PK 3, or 3-km mark).

The best approach to locating both Barau's and Mascarene Black petrel is to charter a deep-sea fishing vessel from either Saint-Gilles or Saint-Pierre. Hire the craft for the afternoon and early evening (till after sunset), make your way 10–20 km offshore and sail between Saint-Gilles and Saint-Pierre. The two species are especially visible in the one or two hours before sunset. Other seabirds to look out for include Wedge-tailed, Audubon's and Mascarene shearwaters; White-tailed Tropicbird; Lesser Noddy; Sooty, Bridled and Common terns. Barau's Petrel is easily observed from the beach at Saint-Pierre, at the mouth of the Saint-Etienne River. Get to the beach at least an hour before sunset and you will see the birds performing offshore, just beyond the surf zone, or flying high overhead inland.

The Mascarene Swiftlet and Mascarene Paradise Flycatcher are found on Mauritius and Réunion. The former is easily seen on both islands, but Réunion is the better venue for seeing the flycatcher, which is rare on Mauritius.

Rodrigues

Endemic birds: Rodrigues Warbler; Rodrigues Fody.

This rather barren island can be reached by air from Mauritius (there are three scheduled flights a week). It has one hotel, though it is logistically quite feasible to locate both the warbler and the fody in the time it usually takes for the aircraft to refuel and otherwise prepare for the return journey, so there is no real need to overnight. You will need at least two hours. Drive from the airport to the Solitude Forest Station or Cascade Pigeon Valley, forested areas in which the birds can easily be found. If you are staying on Rodrigues, though, it would also be worth investigating the offshore islets of Sable, Cocos and Frigate for their populations of Wedge-tailed Shearwater, White Tern, Common Tern and Lesser Noddy. A boat can be chartered locally.

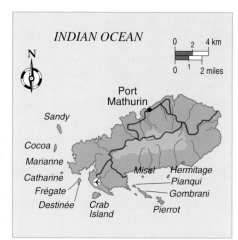

THE SEYCHELLES

CENTRAL SEYCHELLES; ALDABRA ISLANDS.

This island group, renowned as a holiday destination, is well served by international airlines and, moreover, easily reached by air from the Mascarenes and Madagascar. The islands have two main components: first the granitic (or Central) Seychelles, which comprise the rocky group centring on Mahé (largest of the islands), and then the remaining sand- and coral atolls, which stretch from a point north of Mahé to the south and east, almost as far as the Comoros, to a group called the Aldabras. All parts of the Central Seychelles are easily reached either by inter-island ferry or by air (there are daily scheduled flights). Virtually all the endemic birds of the Seychelles group can be seen on the central islands, the more important of which are Mahé, Praslin, La Digue, Cousin and Aride. For especially spectacular tropical seabird sightings, trips to Aride and Bird islands are recommended.

The outlying islands, which are for the most part covered in coconut plantations and are virtually birdless, can be reached either by charter boat or by private (charter) air flights. Some in the Amirante and Farquhar groups are home to spectacular tropical seabird colonies, and

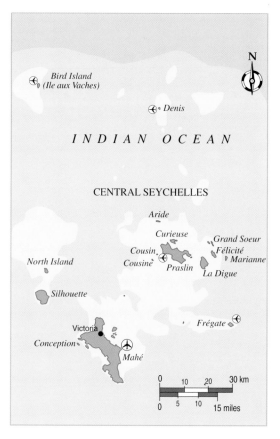

to visit the islands requires special permission. The Aldabras are exceptionally rewarding but access is very difficult: it takes many days to get there by charter boat and there are no aircraft landing facilities. At present, the best option is to visit them is aboard one of the occasional cruise ships, though this is of course an expensive way to see the birds of these biologically exceptional islands.

Central Seychelles
Endemic birds: Seychelles Kestrel; Seychelles Blue Pigeon; Seychelles Black Parrot; Seychelles Scops Owl; Seychelles Swiftlet; Seychelles Bulbul; Seychelles Magpie Robin; Seychelles Brush Warbler; Seychelles Paradise Flycatcher; Seychelles White-eye; Seychelles Sunbird; Seychelles Fody.
The two most difficult species to locate are the scops owl and the white-eye. Seek local assistance for these or concentrate your search in Mahé's Souvenir area and on Conception Island, especially for the Seychelles White-eye. Rewarding trips will be those to La Digue (Paradise Flycatcher), Praslin (Black Parrot) and Aride or Cousin (Magpie Robin and Fody). Seabirds to be seen on Aride, Cousin and Bird islands include Wedge-tailed and Audubon's shearwaters, Red-tailed and White-tailed tropicbirds, Greater and Lesser frigatebirds, Sooty, Bridled, Roseate, White, Greater Crested, and Common and Lesser Noddy terns. A boat trip north of Bird Island and off the archipelago's 'shelf' (20–40 km offshore) might reveal the rarely seen Jouanin's Petrel.

Aldabra Islands
Endemic birds: Aldabra Rail, Aldabra Brush Warbler, Abbott's Sunbird, Aldabra Fody; Aldabra Drongo.
The drongo and fody can easily be located within short walking distance of the research station on Picard Island. For the rail, you will have to visit either Polymnie or Malabar island, to which the bird is confined and where it is common. There are also a few rails on Picard. The brush warbler, on the other hand, has been recorded only from a small area on Malabar and has not been seen since 1983. Among Aldabra's major attractions are the breeding seabirds, and trees that are festooned with Red-footed Boobies and Greater and Lesser frigatebirds – a memorable spectacle. White-tailed and Red-tailed tropicbirds, and Greater-crested, Bridled, Black-naped and White terns also breed here. The very common Abbott's Sunbird is found on nearby Cosmolédo, Astove and Assumption islands, and a special visit to one of them will guarantee sightings of this bird.

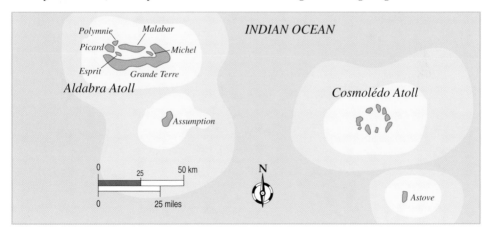

	Abbreviations used in this book		
ad.	adult	br.	breeding	♀	female
juv.	juvenile	non-br.	non-breeding	♂	male

1 ALAOTRA LITTLE GREBE
Tachybaptus rufolavatus ■ 19 cm

In breeding plumage this small, dark-coloured grebe has light tan sides to the neck, a black crown, a pale-yellow eye, and a dark bill with a white tip. Non-br. has a greyish plumage with brownish neck and crown. In breeding plumage, distinguished from Dabchick by its larger size, longer and fairly stout bill and pale eye; and from Madagascar Little Grebe by dark bill, pale eye, tan cheeks. Imm. similar to non-br. ad. Juv. has black and white striping on cheeks and neck. HABITAT Open stretches of fresh water on Lake Alaotra. STATUS Endemic to Madagascar; formerly distributed exclusively on Lake Alaotra, but probably extinct since late 1980s. CALL Unknown.

2 MADAGASCAR LITTLE GREBE
Tachybaptus pelzelnii ■ 19 cm

In breeding plumage this small, dark-coloured grebe has a dark-red eye, pale bill and rufous sides to its neck, separated from the black crown by a white line. Non-br. bird has greyish plumage with brownish neck and crown. In breeding plumage, distinguished from Dabchick by its larger size, longer and lighter-coloured bill, and by the reddish neck separated from brownish crown by a white line. Often found in groups. Imm. similar to non-br. ad. Juv. has black and white striping on cheeks and neck. HABITAT Open stretches of fresh and brackish water, from sea level to high altitude. STATUS Endemic to Madagascar, distributed throughout the island; common. CALL Vocal during breeding season, uttering a noisy, distinctive whinnying trill.

3 DABCHICK (LITTLE GREBE)
Tachybaptus ruficollis ■ 18 cm

In breeding plumage this small, compact, dark-coloured grebe has chestnut sides to the neck, a dark-brown eye, and a yellow patch at the base of the short, straight black bill. Non-br. has greyish plumage with brownish neck. In breeding plumage, distinguished from Madagascar Little Grebe and Alaotra Little Grebe by its smaller size, rufous colour extending to the cheeks, and shorter dark bill with yellow patch at base. Often found in groups. Imm. similar to non-br. ad. Juv. has black and white striping on cheeks and neck. HABITAT Open stretches of fresh and brackish water, from sea level to mid altitude. STATUS Resident on Madagascar and the Comoros. On Madagascar, distributed throughout the island and common; on the Comoros, distributed on Mohéli, Anjouan and Mayotte, and common. CALL Vocal during the breeding season, uttering a noisy whinnying trill.

ad. br.

1

ad. br.

ad. non-br.

ad. br.

2

ad. br.

ad. non-br.

ad. br.

3

ad. br.

ad. non-br.

1 SHY ALBATROSS   *Diomedea cauta* ■ 98 cm
The largest albatross recorded within the area. Differs from both Black-browed
and Yellow-nosed albatrosses in its much paler back and upperwing surface. The
diagnostic underwing flight pattern is wholly white with a very thin black
border. Close observation reveals a clear black 'thumb-print' at the base of the
underwing's leading edge. Varying amounts of grey on the head indicate age, the
darkest grey combined with a greyish collar indicating early immature plumage.
At this age the bird shows a grey bill with a dark tip and, when seen at rest, could
be confused with juv. and imm. Black-browed Albatross. However, the larger size
of this species and its white (not dark) underwing should rule out confusion.
Only the race *salvini* has been recorded from the region. HABITAT Open seas, and
very often close inshore during stormy weather. STATUS Rare winter visitor to the
southern areas of the region; most often seen off southern Madagascar. CALL
Normally silent but utters a loud and raucous 'waaaak' when alarmed.

2 BLACK-BROWED ALBATROSS   *Diomedea melanophris* ■ 90 cm
The adult, with its bright orange bill, is unmistakeable; the bird looks like a huge
Kelp Gull (p. 90), from which it differs in its very long wings, which are held
straight in a powerful gliding flight. Juv. has greyish head and collar with a dark-
tipped grey bill, and closely resembles juv. Shy Albatross but is smaller in size, has
a darker back and upperwings and, most importantly, an almost totally dark (not
white) underwing. Overall, it is bulkier in appearance than both the Shy and the
Yellow-nosed Albatross. It also has a thicker neck, giving it a hunched jizz in
flight. HABITAT Open oceans, rarely venturing close inshore unless blown by
adverse weather. STATUS Uncommon in the southern sector of the region during
winter; seen mostly off southern Madagascar. CALL Usually silent, but it clappers
its bill and grunts when squabbling over food.

3 YELLOW-NOSED ALBATROSS   *Diomedea chlororynchos* ■ 80 cm
Very much smaller and blacker on the back than Shy Albatross. Smaller and more
slender than Black-browed Albatross and differs, at all ages, in the thinner black
border to its underwing, especially on the trailing edge. Further differs from
Black-browed in its juv. plumage, which shows an all-black (not dark-tipped grey)
bill. The all-black bill progressively attains a chrome-yellow ridge on the upper
mandible, which differs markedly from ad. Black-browed Albatross's all-orange
bill. HABITAT Open ocean, but occurs close inshore during storms. STATUS
Uncommon during winter in the southern areas; most frequently seen offshore
in south-east Madagascar. Vagrant to Mascarenes. CALL Usually silent but sometimes clappers its bill and utters a loud, throaty 'weeek'.

4 SOUTHERN GIANT PETREL   *Macronectes giganteus* ■ 90 cm
Occurs in both a white and a dark phase. The former is unmistakeable, the
plumage white with irregular black spots. Dark phase is very variable, plumage
ranging from an overall very dark brown (juv.) through various stages of paler
brown to grey. The most frequently seen are greyish brown with paler grey heads.
A massive, pale-greenish bill is common to all phases and gives the Southern
Giant Petrel a very heavy-headed appearance both in flight and at rest. General
flight action is slow and laboured, and the bird has a peculiar hunched-backed
appearance in flight. HABITAT Open oceans far from land, but will venture close
inshore even during calm weather. STATUS Rare winter visitor to the southernmost
parts of the region. CALL Mostly silent.

1

2

juv.

3

white phase

4

4

dark phase

1 PINTADO PETREL *Daption capense* ■ 40 cm
A pigeon-sized black and white seabird with diagnostic black and white checkered upperparts. Unlikely to be confused with any other seabird in the region. HABITAT Open oceans; rarely inshore during winter. STATUS Uncommon in extreme south and during winter. CALL A high-pitched 'cheecheeecheee' when in feeding groups.

2 BARAU'S PETREL *Pterodroma baraui* ■ 38 cm
In the region, can be confused only with Trinidade and Soft-plumaged petrels. Differs from both in its very obvious white underwing linings bisected by a broad black bar extending from carpals to mid-wing base. At closer range shows black face mask with white forehead; faint open 'M' across back and upperwings. HABITAT Open ocean; closer inshore around Réunion, where it breeds. STATUS Common in seas around Réunion Island and west to Madagascar. CALL Silent at sea.

3 TRINIDADE (ROUND ISLAND) PETREL *Pterodroma arminjoniana* ■ 37 cm
Most closely resembles Barau's Petrel in its pale phase but does not have Barau's striking underwing and head pattern: more uniform brown on head, lacks black mask and white forehead, and has a dusky brown throat and upper breast. In flight shows dark underwings with skua-like white crescents at the primary bases. The bird has an all-dark phase which shows pale wing-patches and, in this plumage, could easily be confused with a dark-phase skua. HABITAT Open oceans, and seas immediately adjacent to Round Island off Mauritius. STATUS Rare and endangered. CALL A harsh 'chuck chuck'.

4 SOFT-PLUMAGED PETREL *Pterodroma mollis* ■ 35 cm
Smaller than both Barau's and Trinidade petrels, with which it could be confused. Differs chiefly in its size and the fairly uniform dark underwing (quite unlike that of Barau's Petrel). At long range can easily be mistaken for Trinidade Petrel pale phase, but lacks that species' conspicuous white wing-flashes. Moreover, flight action more dynamic, with high flying followed by steep and twisting swoops into wave troughs. A very rare dark morph occurs which could be confused with Great-winged and Réunion petrels (p. 38), but its smaller size and overall jizz might help in identification. HABITAT Open seas; rarely seen from shore. STATUS Rare winter visitor to the extreme south of the region. CALL Silent at sea.

5 AUDUBON'S SHEARWATER *Puffinus lherminieri* ■ 28 cm
A tiny black and white shearwater which flies close to the ocean surface with very rapid wing-beats interspersed with short glides. HABITAT Open ocean; close inshore near its breeding areas. STATUS Common to abundant. Breeds on the Comoros, Seychelles and Mascarenes. CALL Silent at sea but gives a shrill squealing sound, often in duet, at night in breeding colonies.

6 MASCARENE SHEARWATER *Puffinus atrodorsalis* ■ 30 cm
Can be confused only with Audubon's Shearwater, from which it differs in its much blacker upperparts and whiter underparts and underwing. Juv. Audubon's of the race *bailloni* is very black above, has white undertail coverts and could easily be mistaken for Mascarene Shearwater. Black on the latter's head ends sharply just below the eye, imparting a strikingly dark-capped appearance. HABITAT Open seas and island coastal waters. STATUS Only recently described. Its breeding islands are not known, but thought to be the Comoros and/or the Mascarenes. CALL Unknown.

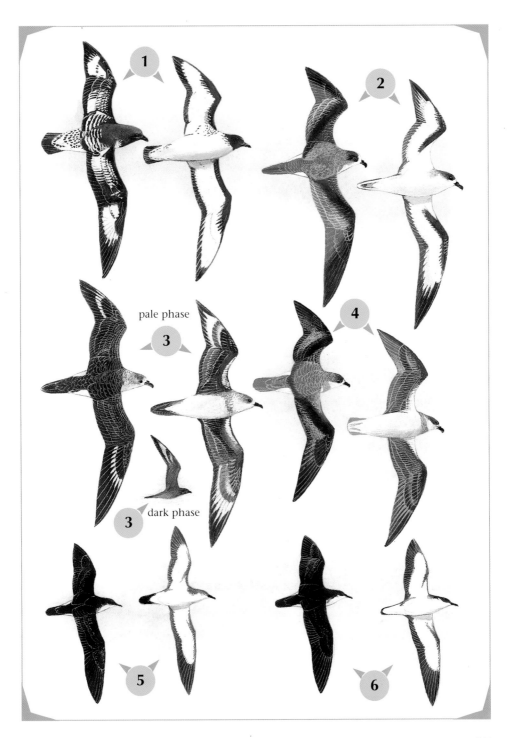

pale phase

dark phase

1 CORY'S SHEARWATER
Calonectris diomedea ∎ 45 cm

Quite unlike any of the region's other seabirds except the Mascarene and Audubon's shearwaters (p. 36), which it dwarfs in size. It also has brown (not black) upperparts. Normal flight slow, low above the water with occasional banking, the wings held stiff and straight. In stronger winds the bird flies faster on flexed wings, with much twisting and banking. HABITAT Open seas; not often seen from shore. STATUS Uncommon summer visitor to southern part of region. CALL Silent at sea.

2 GREAT-WINGED PETREL
Pterodroma macroptera ∎ 42 cm

Easily confused with Réunion Petrel, and with Wedge-tailed and Flesh-footed shearwaters. The bird is larger than Réunion Petrel, and generally paler brown. Flight action is more laboured, with the wings held forward; in calm weather it gives 2–4 quick, stiff wing-beats followed by long glides. Differs from Wedge-tailed Shearwater in its smaller size, and lacks the pointed tail. Its overall shape, with its generally thinner and more flexed wings, is very different from that of the shearwaters with their stiffly held, straight wings. HABITAT Open ocean; very rarely inshore. STATUS Frequent summer visitor to the southern part of the region, but can also be seen north of the tropic. CALL Silent at sea.

3 JOUANIN'S PETREL
Bulweria fallax ∎ 31 cm

Unlikely to be confused with any of the region's other dark seabirds. When seen close to, its pointed tail, pale wing-panels, and pale edging to the secondary coverts are conspicuous. HABITAT Open seas; never seen from land within the region. STATUS Uncertain, but frequently seen within the region during summer, mostly in the northern part. CALL Unknown.

4 RÉUNION PETREL
Pterodroma aterrima ∎ 36 cm

Within the region, the species' range overlaps with, and it is most likely to be mistaken for, the Great-winged Petrel. The Réunion Petrel, however, is noticeably smaller, much darker overall. Flight action is similar to that of the Great-winged Petrel but more agile. HABITAT Open oceans and close to Réunion Island's shore. STATUS Uncertain; uncommon and once thought to be extinct. Almost certainly breeds on Réunion, where it has been found on shore. CALL Unknown.

5 WEDGE-TAILED SHEARWATER
Puffinus pacificus ∎ 45 cm

The region's most abundant dark shearwater. Differs from similar Flesh-footed Shearwater in its pointed (not rounded) tail, and lacks the latter's fleshy white feet. Differs from other dark shearwaters and petrels in its distinctively pointed tail. Jouanin's Petrel shares the latter feature, but that species is very much smaller and has a different flight action. HABITAT Open seas, and close inshore near breeding islands. STATUS Breeds, and is common, throughout region. CALL A wheezing, nasal 'eeh eeh eeh' given at nest burrows, often in a duet.

6 FLESH-FOOTED SHEARWATER
Puffinus carneipes ∎ 45 cm

In colour a warmer, paler brown than Wedge-tailed Shearwater, from which it further differs in its dark-tipped, pale-pink bill which (if seen) is diagnostic. It also lacks Wedge-tailed's pointed tail. Flight action slower, on more flexed wings, than that of the Wedge-tailed Shearwater. HABITAT Open seas; rarely close inshore. STATUS Uncertain. Summer visitor to Mozambique Channel, and recorded south of Madagascar. Most likely overlooked in the region. CALL Silent at sea.

1 WILSON'S STORM PETREL *Oceanites oceanicus* ■ 18 cm
The only storm petrel in the region which has all-dark underparts. This tiny swallow-like seabird is overall sooty black with a wide and contrasting white rump. At close range its long legs can be seen projecting the feet beyond the tail's end, a feature which distinguishes it from, and precludes confusion with, other all-dark storm petrels. Flight is fast on broad, rounded wings, the movement direct with much gliding. When feeding, the bird patters and bounces off the water with its long legs dangling. HABITAT Open seas. STATUS Uncommon all year round but more regularly seen in the winter months, especially in the south of the region. CALL Silent at sea.

2 BLACK-BELLIED STORM PETREL *Fregetta tropica* ■ 20 cm
Easily confused with White-bellied Storm Petrel unless underparts are clearly seen. Overall it appears darker than the White-bellied, and has a wide black stripe that bisects its white belly. It also lacks the scaly upperparts of White-bellied and appears much darker on the back. Flight action is similar in both species: both travel above the waves with erratic changes of direction, sometimes holding still into the wind, their wings flattened, before bouncing off wave-fronts on the breast and belly. HABITAT Open seas. STATUS Uncommon winter visitor throughout the region; mostly seen in the south. CALL Silent at sea.

3 WHITE-BELLIED STORM PETREL *Fregetta grallaria* ■ 20 cm
Very similar to Black-bellied Storm Petrel, and easily confused unless the underparts are clearly seen. This species, however, is overall much paler than the Black-bellied, the scaly pattern on the upperparts reinforcing the paleness. The totally white belly, which extends to the wing lining and over the vent, is very conspicuous and diagnostic. Flight action as in Black-bellied Storm Petrel; both species are often seen riding the bow waves of a ship rather than, as in many other storm petrels, in its wake. HABITAT Open seas. STATUS Uncommon winter visitor throughout the region; mostly seen in the south. CALL Silent at sea.

4 WHITE-FACED STORM PETREL *Pelagodroma marina* ■ 20 cm
This grey and white storm petrel, with its all-white underparts, white face and grey (not white) rump, is unmistakeable. The legs are exceptionally long, the feet projecting well beyond the end of the tail. Flight action is fast and erratic, with constant changes in direction and sometimes with a peculiar buoyant, swinging, to-and-fro motion with legs dangling. HABITAT Open seas; occasionally close inshore, just beyond the reef zone. STATUS Uncertain, but probably more common than is presently recorded. Encountered at sea off northern Madagascar and around the Seychelles. CALL Silent at sea.

1 Red-tailed Tropicbird
Phaethon rubricauda
■ 50 cm (excluding tail streamers)

The adult in breeding season, with its all-white pink-flushed plumage and long red tail-streamers, is unmistakeable. It has a characteristic black lozenge-shaped patch around the eye, and the all-black feet are very often splayed, appearing as black vent against the white plumage. Juv. differs from juv. White-tailed Tropicbird in its larger size, dark (not yellow) bill and more heavily barred upperparts. HABITAT Open oceans, breeding (sometimes in loose colonies) on rocky islands or sandy atolls. STATUS Uncommon throughout the region, with major concentrations in the Seychelles; evenly distributed at sea. CALL A harsh cackling given in flight and from nest.

2 White-tailed Tropicbird
Phaethon lepturus
■ 44 cm (excluding tail streamers)

The smallest and most graceful of all tropicbirds. The adult's totally white plumage is relieved by black wing-tips and a diagonal black bar across the upperwings. Bill is a bright yellow which, at times, can appear orange. Juv. differs from juv. of Red-tailed Tropicbird in its smaller size, greater daintiness in flight, and the greyish appearance of the diagnostic upperwing bar. HABITAT Open seas and rocky islands; prefers to breed in crevices. STATUS The commonest and most frequently encountered tropicbird in the region. CALL A sharp 'kek kek kek' given in flight and from nesting cavities.

3 Greater Frigatebird
Fregata minor ■ 95 cm

The adult male is all-black with a red stripe on throat (only visible at very close range). Similar to the adult male Lesser Frigatebird but the latter has diagnostic white 'armpits'. Female and juv. difficult to tell apart from female and juv. Lesser Frigatebird except under good viewing conditions, when the dark (not pale) 'armpits' are visible. Flight extremely graceful and buoyant with much soaring to great heights. The bird can achieve high speeds in pursuit of terns or boobies. The deeply forked tail is more often held closed and appears thin and pointed. HABITAT Open seas and oceanic islands, where they breed in colonies (Aldabras) or roost in trees. STATUS The species is regularly seen at sea in the more northerly sector of the region. CALL Silent at sea. Displaying males give a whinnying rattle accompanied by bill-clapping.

4 Lesser Frigatebird
Fregata ariel ■ 76 cm

Considerably smaller than Greater Frigatebird, which helps identify the two species in obscure female and juv. plumages, though size is only useful to identification when the two birds are seen together. Ad. male is wholly black with diagnostic white 'armpits'. Female and juv. very variable in plumage combinations but always have white or pale 'armpits'. Males of both species have a red pouch, which they inflate during a bizarre display when at rest or, sometimes, in flight above their breeding areas. HABITAT Open seas and oceanic islands. STATUS Uncommon throughout the region but most frequently seen in the northern parts (breeds on the Aldabra Islands). CALL Whinnying sounds, similar to those of Greater Frigatebird, which it utters in breeding colonies and sometimes in aerial display flight.

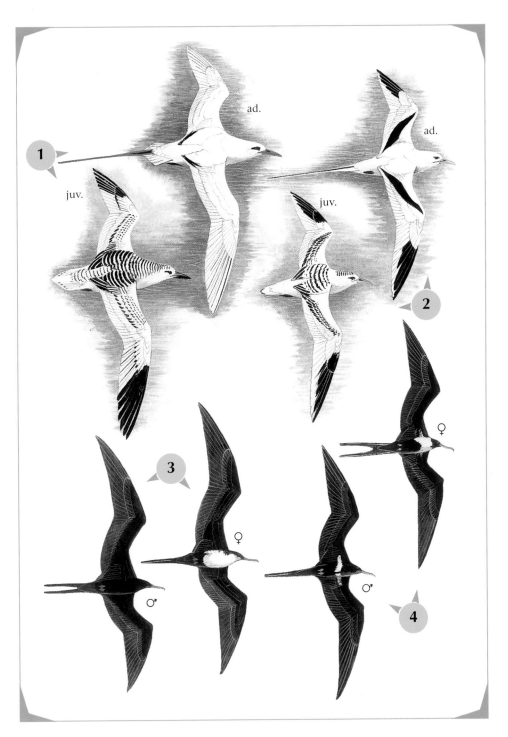

1 REED CORMORANT
Phalacrocorax africanus ■ 55 cm

The region's only cormorant. Not likely to be mistaken for African Darter, which is very much larger and has a long thin neck with a long pointed bill. Ad. in breeding plumage has distinctive crest and yellow-orange facial patch. Juv. is dusky brown with white belly and lacks colour on facial area. HABITAT Very varied, from coastal lagoons and man-made dams to rivers. STATUS Within the region confined to and found throughout Madagascar, where it is represented by the race *pictilis*. CALL Croaking and hissing sounds made at the nest; otherwise silent.

2 AFRICAN DARTER
Anhinga rufa ■ 80 cm

Virtually unmistakeable. When swimming, holds body below water with only the long neck showing, head and bill angled skywards. Juv. is much duller than ad. and has rufous throat and breast. HABITAT Coastal lagoons, mangrove swamps, freshwater lakes and large, slow-moving rivers. STATUS In the region, confined to Madagascar, where represented by the race *vulsini*; most common in island's north and west. CALL Normally silent except when breeding, when it utters croaking noises.

3 RED-FOOTED BOOBY
Sula sula ■ 66–77 cm

The most common booby in the region. Occurs in three colour phases. White phase is easily confused with ad. Masked Booby, but is smaller and more slender and has a white (not black) tail and, if seen, diagnostic red legs and feet. Intermediate and dark phases might be confused with juv. Brown Booby but is more slender and lacks the distinctive pale belly and underwings. Some ad. dark phases are all brown with contrasting white tails. HABITAT Open seas; breeds in the Seychelles group and a few outlying islands. STATUS Often seen in the north and central parts of the region.

4 MASKED BOOBY
Sula dactylatra ■ 81–92 cm

The largest of the boobies, and can be confused only with white phase Red-footed Booby, from which it differs in its black (not white) tail. Juv. very similar to juv. Brown Booby but is larger and has an obvious white collar and pale patch on the back. HABITAT Open seas, often far from breeding islands. STATUS Uncommon in the region's north and east; breeds in the Seychelles and Mascarenes. CALL Hissing and honking noises during display. Silent at sea.

5 BROWN BOOBY
Sula leucogaster ■ 64–74 cm

Adult unmistakeable, with dark-brown plumage relieved only by well-defined white belly and underwings and large pale bill. Juv. shows shadow image of ad. plumage and could be confused with dark or intermediate phase Red-footed Booby but also shows well-marked brown and white (not uniformly brown) underwing plumage. HABITAT Open seas, and close inshore around breeding islands. STATUS Uncommon at sea within the region. Breeds on Seychelles group and Madagascar. CALL Silent at sea, but hisses and honks during display.

6 PINK-BACKED PELICAN
Pelecanus rufescens ■ 140 cm

Unmistakeable, and the only pelican recorded in the region. Juv. is much browner than ad., especially in its first year. Solitary feeder but colonial when breeding. HABITAT Lowland lakes. STATUS Uncertain; used to breed on Madagascar but there have been no records since 1960; could be regionally extinct. CALL Usually silent; various guttural calls when breeding.

ad.

juv.

ad.

ad.

juv.

1

2

light phase

intermediate
phase

dark phase

3

ad.

5

4

juv.

ad.

juv.

juv.

ad.

6

1 MADAGASCAR SQUACCO HERON
Ardeola idae ■ 47 cm

In its breeding plumage this heron is completely white, with a blue, black-tipped bill and pink legs. In non-br. plumage distinguished from Common Squacco Heron by its larger size, stouter bill, much broader streaking on the breast, and the dark-brown mantle and back. HABITAT Mostly freshwater lakes, rivers, marshes and rice paddies but also mangrove stands, seashore and coralline islets. STATUS Breeding endemic to Madagascar and Aldabra, where thinly distributed but can be locally common. Migrant to East Africa. Vagrant to the four islands of the Comoros. CALL A low-pitched, rattling 'kek-kek-kek'.

2 COMMON SQUACCO HERON
Ardeola ralloides ■ 43–46 cm

In breeding plumage, cannot be confused with Madagascar Squacco Heron, which is snow-white. It is overall smaller than the Madagascar Squacco, but differs mainly in its thinner bill, more slender, less robust build and thinner neck. HABITAT Emergent aquatic vegetation around freshwater bodies and large rivers. STATUS Found on Madagascar; common except in the dry south; vagrant to Comoros. CALL Mostly silent, but does utter a low-pitched 'kek kek kek'.

3 LITTLE BITTERN
Ixobrychus minutus ■ 36 cm

Unlikely to be confused with the very similar Yellow Bittern since their ranges do not overlap. Female and juv. duller than male. The bird is most often seen as it flushes from reed beds, flying a short distance before it crashes back into the reeds. HABITAT Mainly in reed beds in freshwater areas. STATUS Confined to Madagascar, where it is uncommon; absent from the south part of the island. CALL A short 'rao' bark given at the onset of breeding.

4 YELLOW (CHINESE) BITTERN
Ixobrychus sinensis ■ 36 cm

A tiny heron found only in the central Seychelles and not likely to be confused with very similar Little Bittern since the two do not occur together. Juv. is duller, lacking buffy panels on the upperwings. Very furtive and not easily seen except when flushed or at first light, when it ventures forth to feed. HABITAT Reed beds surrounding fresh water. STATUS A rare resident, confined to a few islands in the central Seychelles. CALL A soft, guttural grunting.

5 BLACK-CROWNED NIGHT HERON
Nycticorax nycticorax ■ 56 cm

A small, grey and black, stockily built heron which sits hunched up with long white nape plumes spread over the black back. Juv. similar in shape but overall brown with heavy streaking below and white spotting over back. Nocturnal; most often seen by day hiding in tree roosts or venturing forth at dusk. HABITAT Freshwater regions, coastal lagoons and large estuaries. Roosts in dense cover near feeding area. STATUS Confined to Madagascar, where it is common except in the dry south. Vagrant to other islands. CALL Utters a deep, resonant 'gwok' when flying at night from roosting site.

6 GREEN-BACKED (STRIATED) HERON
Butorides striatus ■ 40 cm

The adult is small and dark with bright yellowish-orange legs and feet. Juv. looks like a tiny juv. Black-crowned Night Heron but is much smaller. HABITAT Freshwater bodies, large rivers, mangroves and estuaries. STATUS Occurs within the Seychelles group, Madagascar, Mauritius and Rodrigues. Common in most areas except dry southern Madagascar. CALL When alarmed it utters a short, sharp 'braaek'.

ad. br.

juv.

ad.

juv.

ad. non-br.

ad. non-br.

1

2

♂

♀

♂

♀

3

4

ad.

ad.

juv.

5

6

juv.

1 GREAT WHITE EGRET
Casmerodius albus ■ 92 cm

Altogether much larger than Cattle Egret; also differs from the latter in its very long, thin neck characteristically held in an exaggerated 'S' shape. Differs from Dimorphic Egret which, although similar in shape, is much smaller and has dark legs and contrasting yellow toes. Flight action much slower than that of either Cattle or Dimorphic egret, with slower, more ponderous wing-beats and the legs and feet projecting well beyond tip of tail. HABITAT Freshwater wetlands, larger rivers and estuaries. STATUS Common on Madagascar but rare in the island's dry southern parts. Also found in the Comoros but vagrant to other islands. CALL A low, heron-like 'waaark'.

2 CATTLE EGRET
Bubulcus ibis ■ 54 cm

The adult in breeding plumage differs from Great White Egret and white-phase Dimorphic Egret in the distinctive buff of the crown, back and, sometimes, the breast. Juv. differs from Great White and white-phase Dimorphic egrets in its smaller size, much stockier build and thicker, shorter neck. The Cattle Egret never shows the combination of dark legs and yellow toes of white-phase Dimorphic Egret. HABITAT Usually open fields in association with livestock; not often associated with wetlands. STATUS Common on most islands throughout the region. CALL A typical heron-like 'aaaark' or 'pok pok', uttered mostly in breeding colonies.

3 BLACK EGRET
Egretta ardesiaca ■ 50 cm

May be confused only with dark-phase Dimorphic Egret but differs in its noticeably smaller size, and in the lack of a long, thin neck, white throat and, in flight, white carpal patches. Diagnostic feeding behaviour includes mantling wings over the head. Unlike Dimorphic Egret this species feeds in groups, many birds 'mantling' together in a rice paddy or marsh. HABITAT Freshwater wetlands; rarely saltwater areas. STATUS Confined to Madagascar, where it is common except in the dry southern parts. CALL A deep 'kaark'.

4 DIMORPHIC EGRET
Egretta dimorpha ■ 55–65 cm

Occurs in dark, intermediate and white phases; white phase could be confused with either Great White or juv. Cattle egret. Differs from Cattle Egret in its larger size, its longer, thinner neck, its generally more slender appearance, its thinner and longer bill, and its diagnostic dark legs with yellow toes. Distinguished from Great White Egret by its smaller size, thinner black bill and the diagnostic dark legs with yellow toes. Dark phase closely resembles Black Egret but is much larger and has longer neck, white throat and, in flight, white carpal patches. Should not be confused with Humblot's Heron (p. 50) because, although also very dark in colour, it is totally dwarfed by that species. HABITAT Freshwater wetlands, coastal lagoons and estuaries. STATUS Common on Madagascar and the southern Seychelles; vagrant to other islands. CALL Usually silent, but has a heron-like 'quaark' alarm call.

br.

1

non-br.

br.

2

non-br.

3

light phase

4

dark phase

4

intermediate

49

1 PURPLE HERON
Ardea purpurea ■ 79–91 cm

Smaller than both Grey and Humblot's herons, and also differs from them in its rufous head and neck, and rufous and black underparts. Juv. lacks the grey back of the ad. and is less rufous on the underparts. In flight it is much more slender and streamlined than either Grey or Humblot's heron. On the ground, the head and neck appear very long and thin in profile. HABITAT Frequents those freshwater wetlands surrounded by dense emergent vegetation; less common in open areas and saltwater wetlands. STATUS Confined to and common on Madagascar except for the dry southern parts, where it is rare. Vagrant to other islands in the region. CALL Typical heron-like 'kraaak', most often uttered in flight.

2 GREY HERON
Ardea cinerea ■ 90–100 cm

The most abundant of the region's herons; may be confused only with Purple or Humblot's heron. Differs from former in its overall larger size, grey coloration and the lack of any rufous on head and body. Distinguished from Humblot's by its smaller size, much paler coloration and by the white on its underparts. In flight appears much paler than both Purple and Humblot's herons. HABITAT Both fresh- and saltwater wetlands. STATUS A common resident of Madagascar, the Comoros and Seychelles; vagrant to the Mascarenes. CALL A harsh 'kaarunk' uttered in flight; bill-clapping and guttural noises at nest.

3 HUMBLOT'S HERON
Ardea humbloti ■ 100–110 cm

A large, uniformly dark-grey heron with a black cap and mask, a stout ivory- to orange-coloured bill and a pale-yellow eye. Distinguished from Grey Heron by its larger size and darker plumage with no white showing, and from Purple Heron by its much larger size, black cap and mask and the absence of rufous. Juv. similar to ad. but lacks ornamental feathers and black mask and has a grey bill. HABITAT Freshwater lakes, rivers, rice paddies, mangrove stands, seashore, and coralline islets; from sea level to mid altitude. STATUS Endemic to Madagascar, where it is common. Vagrant to the Comoros (Mohéli, Anjouan and Mayotte). CALL A harsh 'kraaunk' given in flight.

ad.

juv.

1

2

3

1 HAMERKOP
Scopus umbretta ■ 56 cm

This bird, with its curiously shaped head and all-dark brown plumage, is unmistakeable. Usually seen solitary or in pairs, sometimes patrolling roads in search of road-kill amphibians. HABITAT Found chiefly in freshwater wetlands; rarely in salt-water areas. Presence in area often indicated by enormous domed nest of sticks built in tree or on rock face. STATUS In region, confined to Madagascar, where it is common except in the south. CALL A sharp 'kiep' in flight; various querulous squawks and frog-like croaks during display.

2 MADAGASCAR CRESTED IBIS
Lophotibis cristata ■ 50 cm

A large, long-legged, terrestrial forest bird which is quite unmistakeable: it has chestnut colouring, a metallic green crest, a long decurved bill and, in flight, wings that are mostly white. Often found in pairs. Juv. similar to ad. but with smaller crest and dull red bill. HABITAT Dry deciduous and rain forest; from sea level to high altitude. STATUS Endemic to Madagascar, where it is locally common but absent from the south. CALL A guttural 'grow-grow-grow-grow' uttered at night during breeding season.

3 MADAGASCAR SACRED IBIS
Threskiornis bernieri ■ 70–85 cm

A white bird with an unfeathered black head and neck and, seen close to, a pale-blue eye. It has all-white wings without black tips to primaries and secondaries. Juv. has darker-coloured eye, which gradually lightens with age, and black head and neck lightly covered with white and greyish downy feathers. HABITAT Coral lagoons, sandy and muddy intertidal areas and mangroves. STATUS Endemic to the region; found commonly on Aldabra Island and locally on the west coast of Madagascar, where it is uncommon. CALL Various groans, squeaks and hisses, uttered at roosts and in breeding colonies.

4 GLOSSY IBIS
Plegadis falcinellus ■ 65 cm

Unmistakeable, all-dark ibis with a long, decurved bill, slender body on long legs and an oily sheen to plumage. Often forms 'V' formations when flighting to roost or to feeding areas. HABITAT Occurs in most wetlands and recently flooded areas. STATUS In the region confined to Madagascar, where it is locally common but almost absent from the dry south. Vagrant to other islands. CALL Usually silent except in breeding colonies, when it utters a low, guttural 'kok-kok-kok'.

5 AFRICAN SPOONBILL
Platalea alba ■ 90 cm

A large, white, heron-like bird with a distinctively shaped bill (hence the common name). All-white in colour, although when breeding the face and bill ridges become suffused with red. Juv. has a horn-coloured bill. Feeds with characteristic side-to-side sweeping of submerged bill. HABITAT Fresh- and salt-water wetlands. STATUS In this region, confined to Madagascar, where it is locally common. CALL A muffled 'kaaark'; various grunts and bill-clappering when breeding.

juv.

2

ad.

ad.

ad.

3

3

juv.

1

4

5

53

1 YELLOW-BILLED STORK   *Mycteria ibis* ■ 95–105 cm

The region's only black and white stork. Adult has long yellow bill and red face, with a pinkish wash over the mantle when breeding. Juv. is a browner version of ad., the bill a dark horn-colour. In flight, black flight and tail feathers contrast markedly with white plumage. HABITAT Mostly freshwater wetlands, also coastal estuaries and lagoons. STATUS Within the region, known only from Madagascar, where it is locally common, especially in the west. CALL Usually silent except when breeding, when it utters hisses and squeaks at the nest.

2 AFRICAN OPENBILL STORK   *Anastomus lamelligerus* ■ 81–94 cm

The region's only all-black stork. Adult's black plumage has oily sheen and 'wrinkled' feathers on breast. Juv. is duller and lacks fully developed opening between the two mandibles. Like most storks, soars well in flight with neck outstretched and long legs protruding well beyond tail's end. HABITAT Shallow freshwater wetlands; rarely at coastal lagoons and estuaries. STATUS In the region, confined to Madagascar; found in the west of the island, where it is uncommon. CALL Croaking and bill-clappering when alarmed and in breeding colonies.

3 GREATER FLAMINGO   *Phoenicopterus ruber* ■ 124–140 cm

Can be confused only with Lesser Flamingo, with which it often associates. Greater is very much the taller of the two, is overall less pink and has a diagnostic dark-tipped pink bill. Juv. is a dull greyish-brown version of the ad. and has a dark-tipped whitish bill, which distinguishes it from imm. Lesser Flamingo. In flight shows much more pink on wings than is evident when at rest. HABITAT Coastal lagoons, estuaries, salt pans and brackish lakes. STATUS The species breeds on Madagascar and occasionally on Aldabra Island. Vagrant elsewhere in the region. On Madagascar, confined to the west and south. CALL Various goose-like honkings.

4 LESSER FLAMINGO   *Phoenicopterus minor* ■ 80–100 cm

Differs from Greater Flamingo in its obviously smaller size (evident when the two are seen together) and overall much pinker colour, especially in breeding plumage. The deep red bill (as against the dark-tipped pink of the Greater Flamingo) is diagnostic. At a distance the bill appears black. Juv. differs from juv. Greater Flamingo in its smaller size and all-dark bill. Often found alongside Greater Flamingo, but forages in deeper water, sometimes swimming with head held below surface. HABITAT Brackish coastal lakes, freshwater lakes, salt pans and estuaries. STATUS Locally common on Madagascar; vagrant to other islands; does not breed in the region. CALL Goose-like honking, similar to that of Greater Flamingo.

ad.

juv.

1

2

ad.

ad.

3

ad.

4

ad.

ad.

juv.

juv.

1 BERNIER'S TEAL
Anas bernieri ■ 45 cm

A medium-sized, light-brown, surface-feeding duck with a reddish bill and legs. In flight its conspicuous blue speculum is framed with white, and it also shows a partly white underwing. Distinguished from Red-billed Teal by the less contrasting colours of the head, duller red bill and, in flight, by the blue speculum. Found in small groups. Male slightly larger than female. Juv. differs from ad. in its duller plumage. HABITAT Freshwater but more often brackish lakes and mangrove stands close to and at sea level. STATUS Endemic to Madagascar; occurs in the west, where it is rare. CALL Unknown.

2 RED-BILLED TEAL
Anas erythrorhyncha ■ 43–48 cm

Can be confused with both Bernier's and Hottentot teals. Paler below than the former, with a more obvious and contrasting dark cap and red (not reddish brown) bill. In flight shows pale wingbar instead of Bernier's pale bordered speculum. Sits higher in water than Bernier's. Hottentot Teal is much smaller and has dark smudge on cheek, and a blue (not red) bill. HABITAT Occurs in most wetlands from saline coastal regions to lakes and even fast-flowing rivers. STATUS In the region, confined to Madagascar where it is the most common of the ducks. CALL Male gives a nasal whistle; the female quacks.

3 GARGANEY
Anas querquedula ■ 38 cm

The male has an obvious broad, white eye-stripe on its dark-brown head, which in itself should rule out confusion with any of the region's other ducks. Moreover, the brown breast ends abruptly and is finely demarcated. Female and juv. more obscure and could possibly be confused with other teals, but the species lacks the dark caps of the other birds and, in flight, shows a powder-blue forewing. HABITAT Virtually any freshwater environment except fast-flowing rivers. STATUS Uncommon summer visitor to the Mascarenes and Seychelles. CALL A nasal quack and softer rattling noises.

4 HOTTENTOT TEAL
Anas hottentota ■ 35 cm

The smallest teal in the region, which helps distinguish it from Bernier's and Red-billed teals. Further differs by showing obvious dark smudge on buffy cheeks and a blue (not red) bill. In flight shows a white trailing edge to the wings and a black and white underwing pattern. HABITAT Prefers wetlands with floating vegetation and cover. STATUS In the region, confined to Madagascar; more common in the west, uncommon elsewhere. CALL Soft quacking noises.

5 MELLER'S DUCK
Anas melleri ■ 55 cm

A large, brown, surface-feeding duck with a long, greyish-blue bill and orange legs. In flight it displays a conspicuous metallic green or blue speculum and white underwing. Often found in pairs. Distinguished from female domestic mallards by its larger size, darker plumage and greyish-blue bill. Male slightly larger than female. Juv. similar to ad. but with a darker bill and duller, brownish plumage. HABITAT Lakes, rivers, marshes with open water; from sea level to high altitude. STATUS Endemic to Madagascar; occurs (uncommon) on the high central plateau and in the east; and occasionally on major lakes in the west. Introduced to Mauritius, where it is rare. CALL A guttural 'kakakaka' occasionally uttered.

1 FULVOUS DUCK
Dendrocygna bicolor ■ 43–50 cm

Similar to White-faced Duck, from which it is distinguished by the golden brown (not white) face. The Fulvous Duck is overall more rufous, with broad white striping on flanks. Confusion most likely with juv. White-faced Duck, which in fact does not have a white face but is greyish brown (not rufous) on head. HABITAT Freshwater wetlands; more rarely in coastal saline areas. STATUS In the region, occurs only on Madagascar, where it is locally common in the north and west. CALL A harsh, rasping, two-note whistle.

2 WHITE-FACED DUCK
Dendrocygna viduata ■ 43–53 cm

The only duck in the region with a white face, although this is invariably stained with mud and may not be immediately obvious. The species differs from similar-shaped Fulvous Duck in its darker overall colouring, the lack of broad white flank-stripes, and in its chestnut (not rufous) breast. HABITAT Various wetlands and flooded areas, but unusual in saltwater areas. STATUS Common and sometimes abundant on Madagascar. Vagrant to other islands. CALL An often repeated tri-syllabic whistle.

3 KNOB-BILLED DUCK
Sarkidiornis melanotos ■ 56–76 cm

The region's largest and only black and white duck. Male much larger than female and in breeding season has an extended black disc on upper mandible. In non-br. season the disc is much reduced. Female and juv. have white bodies and heads, which contrast with black wings, back and tail. HABITAT Freshwater wetlands and lakes. STATUS In the region, found only on Madagascar, where locally common. CALL Mostly silent, but utters a wheezy whistle in flight.

4 MADAGASCAR POCHARD
Aythya innotata ■ 45 cm

A chestnut-brown diving duck with white undertail coverts and a pale eye. On water it sits low with tail submerged. In flight displays a dark wing with conspicuous white bar and black-tipped flight feathers. Female has dark eye and is a duller brown, lacking the chestnut of the male. Juv. similar to ad. female. HABITAT Freshwater reaches of Lake Alaotra. STATUS Endemic to Madagascar and, when extant, distributed exclusively on Lake Alaotra, with a few seen on lakes near Antananarivo. Not seen since early 1990s. CALL Unknown.

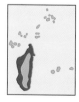

5 WHITE-BACKED DUCK
Thalassornis leuconotus ■ 38–40 cm

An oddly shaped duck, with angular head; sits very low in water imparting a hunch-backed appearance. Mottled brown and buff without any diagnostic features when at rest except for a fairly inconspicuous white oval patch at base of bill. Reluctant to fly but when flushed it patters clumsily over the water, showing the diagnostic white stripe down its back. HABITAT Wetlands with floating vegetation, especially waterlilies. STATUS In the region, found only on Madagascar, where generally uncommon. CALL A low-pitched whistle, rising toward the end.

6 PYGMY GOOSE
Nettapus auritus ■ 33 cm

This tiny duck, with its brightly coloured green and chestnut plumage, is unmistakeable. Male has brighter coloured head than female and juv. In flight, which is very fast, shows diagnostic white speculum. HABITAT Freshwater wetlands with floating vegetation. STATUS In the region, occurs only on Madagascar, where it is locally common in the west but rarer elsewhere and almost absent from the south. CALL A soft, repeated 'tsui tsui' uttered in flight.

1 Madagascar Fish Eagle
Haliaeetus vociferoides ■ 70–80 cm

A very large, brown raptor with long rounded wings and a square white tail, white cheeks and whitish sides to the neck. Overall impression in flight is of a big, broad-winged eagle with a short tail. Distinguished from all other raptors by its large size, the shape of its wings and the colour of its tail. Female slightly larger than male. Juv. and imm. differ from ad. in their generally duller brownish plumage, light brown heads with whitish cheeks, and greyish tails with a dark terminal band. HABITAT Lakes, rivers, sometimes marshes with open waters, fringes of natural forest, mangrove stands, rocky coastline and offshore islets; from sea level to mid altitude. STATUS Endemic to Madagascar; distributed on the west coast up to 100 km inland; uncommon. CALL Very vocal; call comprises a ringing 'kyow-koy-koy-koy' uttered from perch or in flight. Pairs often duet.

2 Madagascar Serpent Eagle
Eutriorchis astur ■ 66 cm

A large, brown forest raptor with barred underparts and tail. Distinguished from Henst's Goshawk by its larger size, brown upperparts, broader breast-barring, short but obvious crest, and short, yellow legs. Differs from juv. and imm. Madagascar Harrier Hawk by barred chest and belly. In flight it has rounded wings and a long barred tail. Juv. and imm. differ from ad. in the pale edging of feathers on their head, shoulders and back. HABITAT Rain forest from sea level to mid altitude. STATUS Endemic to Madagascar, where it is confined to the east; rare and secretive. CALL A slowly repeated, deep and throaty 'how-how-how-how' given from a perch, and a more rapid 'kooa-kooa-kooa' uttered in flight when leaving a perch.

3 Henst's Goshawk
Accipiter henstii ■ 52–62 cm

A medium-sized to large, dark-brown forest raptor with barred underparts. Distinguished from Madagascar Serpent Eagle by its smaller size, the pale stripe above the eye, thinner breast-bars, darker upperparts and long, yellow legs. Distinguished from other accipiters by larger size and darker plumage. In flight it has rounded wings, a long, barred tail and a pale rump. Female distinctly larger than male. Juv. differs from ad. in its brown upperparts and the large brown spots on its breast and belly. HABITAT Rain forest and deciduous dry forest; from sea level to high altitude. STATUS Endemic to Madagascar; distributed in the east and the west; uncommon throughout its range. CALL Fairly vocal in the breeding season; utters a loud, rapid 'keey-keey-keey-keey-keey' while perched or in flight.

4 Madagascar Harrier Hawk
Polyboroides radiatus ■ 68 cm

A very large grey raptor with wide, rounded grey wings edged with black, a long black tail barred with white, and yellow or pink facial skin. Perched on or above the ground it displays a typically slender silhouette with long, thin, yellow legs. Distinguished from all other raptors by the shape of the wings, general grey coloration and the colour of the tail. Juv. distinguished from Madagascar Serpent Eagle and Henst's Goshawk by its whitish head with black mask, and plain brownish breast and belly. Juv. differs from ad. in its generally dull, brownish plumage showing a scaly pattern, and in its whitish head. HABITAT A wide variety of forest habitat from sea level to high altitude. STATUS Endemic to Madagascar; distributed throughout the island, where it is common. CALL Very vocal species with a diagnostic high-pitched, shrill 'peee-eee-ooo-ooo' call uttered from a perch or in flight.

ad. (not to scale)

ad.

1

1

juv.

ad.

2

ad.

2

juv.

ad.

3

ad.

3

juv.

ad.

ad.

4

juv.

1 Madagascar Buzzard
Buteo brachypterus ■ 48–51 cm

A medium-sized brown raptor with short, rounded wings and open, fan-shaped tail. Plumage subject to considerable variation, some individuals showing a variable amount of white on the breast, belly and rump. Overall impression in flight is of a short-winged raptor with barred underwings and tail. Similar to Madagascar Cuckoo Hawk but distinguished by its larger head, broader wings, longer whitish legs, short rounded tail and generally whitish belly. Juv. differs from ad. in its light-coloured eye. HABITAT A very wide variety of forest habitat; open savanna areas near forest edge; rocky outcrops; from sea level to high altitude. STATUS Endemic to Madagascar; distributed throughout the island, where it is common. CALL Very vocal species with a characteristically piercing, plaintive 'pe-ooooo' mew uttered from a perch or in flight.

2 Madagascar Cuckoo Hawk
Aviceda madagascariensis ■ 40–45 cm

A medium-sized brown raptor with rather long, narrow wings, a long, slightly notched tail and a pale rump. Similar to the Madagascar Buzzard but distinguished by its small head, pale, bulging eyes, narrower wings, long, narrow and slightly notched tail, and brownish belly contrasting with whitish breast, and has shorter legs. Juv. differs from ad. in its brown eyes. HABITAT A large variety of forest habitat, from sea level to mid altitude. STATUS Endemic to Madagascar; distributed throughout the island, where it is uncommon. CALL Unknown.

3 Réunion Harrier
Circus maillardi ■ 54–59 cm

A large raptor with a slender silhouette and a long tail. The bird displays a typically slow, buoyant flight a few metres off the ground. Male easily identifiable by its blackish back and head and white belly, which contrasts with the grey and black wings and unbarred tail. Female and juv. are dark brown with white rump and barred tail. The subspecies *macrosceles* of Madagascar and Comoros is considered a separate species by some authorities. HABITAT Both dry and flooded grasslands; marshes. STATUS Endemic to the region; restricted to Madagascar (uncommon), Réunion (common) and the Comoros, found on the four main islands and uncommon except on Mayotte, where it is rare. CALL Vocal near breeding site, where it utters a piercing 'kay keyk-key-key'.

4 Black Kite
Milvus migrans ■ 56 cm

Can be confused only with juv. Yellow-billed Kite but is overall much paler, especially on the head. Also differs in its smaller, more compact bill and pale eye. It is doubtful, however, whether juv. Yellow-billed and Black kites can be clearly distinguished in the field. HABITAT Diverse; virtually any environment, but avoids densely forested areas. STATUS Uncertain, but has been identified in the dry south of Madagascar during summer. CALL Silent outside breeding cycle.

5 Yellow-billed Kite
Milvus aegyptius ■ 56 cm

The adult is large and easily identified, and has a diagnostic yellow bill. Differs from Black Kite in its overall darker coloration and, especially, its darker head. Juv. can be confused with ad. Black Kite but is darker, lacks pale eye and paler streaked head. Juvs. of the two species probably indistinguishable in the field. HABITAT Wide-ranging, present in virtually all habitats but has preference for wetter areas; avoids densely wooded regions. STATUS Occurs throughout the year in Madagascar and the Comoros; common. Probable vagrant to Seychelles but not specifically identified. CALL A high-pitched, shrill whinnying.

ad.

juv.

63

1 BANDED KESTREL   *Falco zoniventris* ■ 35 cm
A medium-sized falcon with grey upperparts, pale underparts heavily streaked on the throat and upper breast, and barred on lower breast and belly with dark grey; pale-yellow eye surrounded by bare yellow skin. Distinguished from other falcons by the bars on its breast and belly and its yellow eye. Juv. differs from ad. in its brown (not grey) upperparts, darker eye, and smaller bare eye-patch. HABITAT A very wide variety of forest habitat, especially forest edge and clearings; from sea level to mid altitude. STATUS Endemic to Madagascar and distributed throughout the island, but uncommon. CALL Not very vocal outside breeding season, when it utters a high-pitched 'kik-kik-kik'.

2 MADAGASCAR SPARROWHAWK   *Accipiter madagascariensis* ■ 34–40 cm
A medium-sized, dark-grey forest raptor with dark-grey barred underparts and a long, dark-grey barred tail. Distinguished from Henst's Goshawk (p. 60) by smaller size and thinner bars on breast and belly, and from Frances's Sparrowhawk by its larger size, darker upperparts and darker bars on the breast and belly. Female larger than male, with dark-brown bars on the breast and belly. Juv. differs from ad. in its brown upperparts and spotted underparts. HABITAT Rain forest, deciduous dry forest and subarid thorn scrub. STATUS Endemic to Madagascar; found throughout the island; uncommon. CALL A high pitched 'kee-kee-kee-kee'.

3 FRANCES'S SPARROWHAWK   *Accipiter francesiae* ■ 30–35 cm
A small, slender sparrowhawk with blue-grey upperparts, almost white underparts variably barred with pale rufous, and a blue-grey tail barred with dark grey. Distinguished from other accipiters by its smaller size, almost-white breast and belly, and grey back and mantle. Female distinguished from ad. Banded Kestrel by its more slender silhouette, brown plumage, and longer legs. Female larger than male, with brown upperparts and pale underparts barred with brown. Juv. differs from ad. in its brown upperparts and spotty underparts. HABITAT Rain forest, deciduous dry forest, subarid thorn scrub, exotic wood plantations and gardens; from sea level to high altitude. STATUS Endemic to Madagascar (common), Grande Comore (common), Anjouan (rare), and Mayotte (common). CALL Not very vocal outside the breeding season, when it utters a high-pitched 'kee-kee-kee'.

4 BAT HAWK   *Macheiramphus alcinus* ■ 45 cm
Can be confused with Sooty and dark-phase Eleonora's falcons (p. 66) but is larger has much broader wings, shorter tail and very different flight action. Flight appears languid and leisurely, but when in pursuit of bats or birds, it is very fast, characterized by twists and turns and rapid stoops. HABITAT Woodland, with nearby open grasslands and often close to villages. STATUS In the region, confined to Madagascar, where it is rare. CALL Utters a high-pitched whistling sound when breeding.

5 PEREGRINE FALCON   *Falco peregrinus* ■ 33–46 cm
Can be confused with Eleonora's and Sooty falcons (p. 66). When seen clearly the black mask with tear-drop and the finely grey-barred underparts are diagnostic. Lacks rusty coloration on underparts of Eleonora's Falcon in all plumages, and never shows the latter's all-dark underwing. HABITAT Breeds in rocky and mountainous areas but found virtually everywhere except dense forest. STATUS Occurs on Madagascar and the Comoros; uncommon. Vagrant to Seychelles. CALL A raucous 'kak-kak-kak-kak-kak' uttered around nest.

1 SEYCHELLES KESTREL
Falco araea ■ 15–23 cm

The only kestrel found in the central Seychelles. A small falcon, ad. with uniform (not spotted) underparts; juv. spotted and streaked on underparts. Solitary; sometimes seen in pairs; uses a regular hunting or lookout perch. Does not hunt in usual kestrel hovering fashion but grabs prey from perched position. Will soar on thermals above its territory. HABITAT Found in various degraded wooded areas and among rock faces. STATUS Endemic to central Seychelles; common on Mahé; less so on neighbouring islands. CALL A thin, mewing 'ti ti ti ti'.

2 MADAGASCAR KESTREL
Falco newtoni ■ 25–30 cm

A small falcon with a grey head, rufous upperparts and wings, whitish underparts, and a grey tail barred with black. This is the region's only falcon that habitually hovers. Female has a tan head, speckled upperparts and underparts, and a brown tail. Juv. differs from ad. in its buff-edged flight feathers and its more heavily streaked underparts. A minority (about 20%) of the birds show a rufous morph, in which males display a rufous breast, belly and back and darker head and neck. This morph is restricted largely to Madagascar's high central plateau. HABITAT A wide variety of open habitats, including human settlement, grassland, wooded savanna and rocky outcrops; avoids dense forest. Found from sea level to high altitude. STATUS Endemic to the region; found throughout Madagascar, where it is common; and on Aldabra, where it is uncommon. CALL Vocal; utters a typical high-pitched 'kikik-kikik-kikik' from a perch or in flight.

3 MAURITIUS KESTREL
Falco punctatus ■ 20–26 cm

The only small falcon to be found on Mauritius. Female slightly larger than male. Juv. has bluish facial skin which gradually turns yellow with age. Prefers to hunt from a perch but will soar above its territory and has been seen to hover in more open areas. HABITAT Occurs in remnant patch of natural forest in south-west Mauritius; has been successfully introduced to secondary growth in other parts of the island. STATUS Endemic to Mauritius, where its population has been built up from a handful to more than 50 breeding pairs. CALL A 'too-ee' whistling note.

4 ELEONORA'S FALCON
Falco eleonorae ■ 36–40 cm

Can be confused with Peregrine Falcon (p. 64) and Sooty Falcon. Dark phase differs from former in its larger size, broader-based wings with much darker underwings, and, when seen close, the male's greenish (not chrome-yellow) cere, legs and feet. Female has blue cere. Smaller than Peregrine with proportionately longer wings and tail, and shows rusty or rufous on underparts in all plumages. HABITAT Forests and wooded savanna, often close to wetlands. STATUS Common summer visitor to the region, mostly to Madagascar. CALL Silent in the region.

5 SOOTY FALCON
Falco concolor ■ 32–36 cm

Can be confused with larger dark-phase Eleonora's Falcon but is smaller and much more slender, longer-tailed and winged and very much more buoyant and agile in flight. Female and juv. much larger than Madagascar Kestrel and very different in shape. Differs from similar-plumaged Eleonora's Falcon in its size, shape and buffier (not so rufous) underparts. Very rapid in flight; angled wings and long, slightly pointed tail give the impression of an over-sized swift. HABITAT Wooded areas and open grasslands, often near water. Sometimes seen hawking above canopy. STATUS Common summer visitor to Madagascar. Vagrant to all other island groups. CALL Silent in the region.

♂

1

♂

1

♀

2

pale phase

dark phase

2

juv.

3

ad. ♂

ad. ♂

3

juv.

ad. ♂

ad.
pale phase

4

4

ad. dark phase

juv.

ad. ♂
(pale)

5

5

ad. ♀
(dark)

juv.

1 GREY FRANCOLIN   *Francolinus pondicerianus* ■ 33–35 cm

The only francolin found in the region. A small, finely barred gamebird with a chestnut throat. Very furtive, preferring to run and hide but, when disturbed, bursts from cover with rapid, clapping wing-beats. HABITAT Scrub thickets in grassy and lightly wooded areas. STATUS Introduced to and still extant on Mascarenes and Seychelles. CALL A high-pitched chicken-like 'claaaak'.

2 HARLEQUIN QUAIL   *Coturnix delegorguei* ■ 16 cm

The male is striking in appearance, with chestnut and black underparts and a distinctive black and white throat pattern. Female and juv. unlikely to be told apart from similar Common Quail. Like Common Quail, the bird flushes from grass cover and dashes off at great speed in direct flight. HABITAT Grasslands with scanty bush cover. STATUS Uncommon breeding summer visitor to Madagascar. CALL Similar to that of Common Quail but notes higher pitched and more metallic.

3 MADAGASCAR PARTRIDGE   *Margaroperdix madagascariensis* ■ 24–26 cm

This bird's large size, black and white mask, black throat, buff chest and black belly, which is marked with very large white spots, are all diagnostic. Often found in pairs or small groups. Male slightly larger than female, which is tan-brown with dark-brown stripes on the upperparts and large scallops on the underparts. Juv. is duller. HABITAT Grassland, forest edge and forest clearing. STATUS Endemic to Madagascar; common. Introduced to Réunion (common) and Mauritius (uncommon). CALL Fairly silent except for short, throaty contact calls.

4 COMMON QUAIL   *Coturnix coturnix* ■ 17 cm

A small, rotund, terrestrial bird which could be confused with Harlequin Quail, but lacks the latter's striking chestnut-coloured underparts and black and white throat pattern. Females of the two species very similar. Most often encountered as it 'explodes' from cover and makes off on whirring wings in fast and direct flight. HABITAT Grasslands. STATUS Breeds on Madagascar, where it is locally common. Vagrant to Comoro Islands; introduced to Mascarenes. CALL Utters a 'crwee-crwee' in flight, but the bird's usually cryptic presence is more often revealed by its 'wit wit-wit' call.

5 BLUE-BREASTED QUAIL   *Coturnix chinensis* ■ 15 cm

The male bird, with its black and white throat pattern and blue and chestnut underparts, is unmistakeable. Female could be confused with Common Quail but is very much smaller. Female might also just be mistaken for similar-sized female Madagascar Button-Quail (p. 70) but is distinguished by its rust-coloured face and breast, fine black cheek-stripe and fine black barring on belly and flanks. HABITAT Damp grassy areas and thicket. STATUS Introduced to the Mascarenes; uncommon on Réunion; now extinct on Mauritius. CALL A two-syllable 'ti-yu'.

6 HELMETED GUINEAFOWL   *Numida meleagris* ■ 58–64 cm

Unmistakeable. Juv. has less-developed casque than ad. Male has longer casque than female. Flies strongly when flushed, often over long distance. Roosts in trees and bushes, sometimes high up in canopy. Very furtive and wary, associating in small groups. Domesticated birds often show blotchy white feathering. HABITAT Mostly open grasslands; also lightly wooded areas and cultivated lands. STATUS Introduced to Madagascar and Comoros; uncommon and localized. CALL A repetitive 'krrdii-krrddii' crowing; alarm note a sharp 'kek kek kek'.

1 MADAGASCAR WOOD RAIL   *Canirallus kioloides* ■ 28 cm
Distinguished from White-throated Rail (p. 72) by its smaller size, grey head, dark undertail coverts and short, straight bill, and from Brown Mesite by its heavier appearance, short tail, grey head and white throat. HABITAT Undisturbed rain forest and locally deciduous dry forest; from sea level to mid altitude. STATUS Endemic to Madagascar; found in the east and in the north-west and common, as well as locally in one site in the west. CALL Fairly vocal, uttering a loud, piercing whistle with rising inflection.

2 BROWN MESITE   *Mesitornis unicolor* ■ 30 cm
A plain rufous-brown terrestrial species with a short, straight bill, short legs and a rather long tail. Very secretive. Distinguished from Madagascar Flufftail (p. 72) by its larger size, stretched-out silhouette and long tail; from Madagascar Wood Rail by its slimmer silhouette and brownish head and throat; and from the White-breasted Mesite by its plain brown plumage and shorter bill. Usually found alone or in pairs. HABITAT Undisturbed rain forest. STATUS Endemic to Madagascar; distributed across the east of the island, where it is uncommon. CALL Fairly vocal species during breeding season, uttering a loud, whistling 'oohcoo-oohcoo-oohcoo' repeated several times. Breeding pairs often sing in duet.

3 WHITE-BREASTED MESITE   *Mesitornis variegata* ■ 31 cm
A terrestrial species with a characteristically slender, horizontal silhouette, fairly long tail, short legs, grey and brown upperparts, white breast and belly with black dots, and a conspicuous creamy supercilium. A secretive species, usually found in pairs or small groups. Juv. similar to ad. but duller with a yellow-buff throat and supercilium. HABITAT Deciduous dry forest; very locally in rain forest; from sea level to low altitude. STATUS Endemic to Madagascar. Patchily distributed along the west coast in four different locations, and in one site in the rain forest of the east coast. CALL Vocal species during the breeding season, when it utters a loud, modulated 'wee-hoo-wee-hoo' whistle repeated several times. Pairs often sing in duet. Contact call a soft 'see-see-see', often heard when feeding.

4 SUBDESERT MESITE   *Monias benschi* ■ 32 cm
A terrestrial species with grey plumage above, white below with black dots on the breast, a conspicuous white supercilium, longish decurved bill, and rather long, graduated tail. Female has extensive rufous throat and breast. HABITAT Spiny bush forest near sea level. STATUS Endemic to Madagascar; found in the south-west along a narrow coastal strip. CALL A vocal species during the breeding season, uttering a crescendo of 'tse-tse-tse-tse' notes. Breeding pairs often sing in duet.

5 MADAGASCAR BUTTON-QUAIL   *Turnix nigricollis* ■ 14–16 cm
This bird can be distinguished from Common and Harlequin quails (p. 68) by its small size, black throat and breast (female), deep-rufous shoulder patch (female) and light yellow eye, all of which are diagnostic. Female larger and brighter than male, which lacks the black throat and rufous breast and shows a tan-grey plumage. Female distinguished from females of Common Quail and Harlequin Quail by its smaller size, pale eye and bill and with underparts finely barred on breast and belly. Juv. differs from ad. in its smaller size and more rufous wings. HABITAT Grassland, dry fields, forest; from sea level to high altitude. STATUS Endemic to Madagascar; common. Introduced to Réunion and Mauritius, where common. CALL A low-pitched 'bub-bub-bub', discernible only when close by.

1 ALDABRA RAIL   *Dryolimnas aldabranus* ■ 28–30 cm

A medium-sized, flightless rail with a rufous head, white throat, greenish upper-parts, white undertail coverts, a long, blackish bill with a dark-red base, and long, blackish legs. Very similar to White-throated Rail. Silhouette is slim. Found alone or in pairs, often seen in the open. Female differs from male in the bright pink base to its bill. Juv. differs from ad. mainly in its brownish plumage. HABITAT Mangrove stands, woodlands, wetlands and beaches. STATUS Endemic to Aldabra, where it is common. CALL Very vocal, uttering a strikingly loud, piercing 'chee-ee chee-ee chee-ee' whistle which rises and falls on the scale.

2 WHITE-THROATED RAIL   *Dryolimnas cuvieri* ■ 31 cm

A medium-sized rail easily distinguished from the Madagascar Wood Rail (p. 70) by its larger size, large white throat, rufous head, long red bill, white undertail coverts and slimmer silhouette; and from the Madagascar Rail by its larger size, and blackish belly and thighs showing thin white barring. Found singly or in pairs; often seen in the open. Rarely flies. Juv. differs from ad. mainly in its brownish plumage and black bill. HABITAT Wetlands, rice paddies, mangrove stands, woodland watercourses. STATUS Endemic to Madagascar; common throughout island. CALL Vocal, uttering a loud, piercing 'wee-you-wee-you-wee-you' whistle. Individuals respond to each other's calls.

3 SLENDER-BILLED FLUFFTAIL   *Sarothrura watersi* ■ 15 cm

A very small rail. The male's generally rufous-brown plumage, which lacks black marks, and its larger size distinguish it from the male of Madagascar Flufftail. The rufous underparts, including the undertail coverts, distinguish it from Baillon's Crake (p. 74). The female is plain fawn in colour except for its streaked undertail coverts. Its larger size and plain-coloured breast and belly distinguish it from female of Madagascar Flufftail. Juv. unknown. HABITAT Marshes at the edge of rain forest; from mid to high altitude. STATUS Endemic to Madagascar; distributed in a few localities in the east, where it is rare. CALL Vocal during the breeding season, uttering a low, deep, rapid, and constant 'gu-duk gu-duk gu-duk'.

4 MADAGASCAR RAIL   *Rallus madagascariensis* ■ 25 cm

A medium-sized aquatic rail, distinguished from the White-throated Rail by its smaller size, slimmer silhouette, grey face and throat, purple underparts, and long curved bill. Secretive and shy; found singly or in pairs; rarely seen in the open. Juv. duller than ad. HABITAT Wetlands with dense vegetation. STATUS Endemic to Madagascar; distributed in the east, where it is uncommon. CALL Vocal; utters a loud 'klee killee klee' during the day from dense vegetation.

5 MADAGASCAR FLUFFTAIL   *Sarothrura insularis* ■ 14 cm

A very small rail. The male's rufous head and breast are diagnostic, distinguishing it from the males of Baillon's Crake (p. 74) and Slender-billed Flufftail. Female's plumage is fawn heavily streaked with black; streaked underparts distinguish it from female of Slender-billed Flufftail. Female distinguished from male of Madagascar Button-Quail (p. 70) by its smaller size, dark bill and eye and fluffy tail. HABITAT Grassland, edges of rain forest, clearings, undisturbed and secondary rain forest; from sea level to very high altitude. STATUS Endemic to Madagascar; distributed in the east, where it is common. CALL Very vocal, uttering a loud, piercing, descending 'bee-bee-bee-bee-beeree-beeree-beeree-be-be-be' whistle. Individuals respond to each other's calls.

(short bill)

73

1 BAILLON'S CRAKE
Porzana pusilla ■ 16–18 cm

A tiny crake which, if only briefly seen, might be mistaken for Slender-billed Flufftail (p. 72), which sometimes shares the same habitat. The crake is larger and is overall greyish in appearance with fairly conspicuous grey underparts and black and white barred flanks. Juv. is duller than ad. and has paler underparts but still shows barred flanks. HABITAT Wetlands with ample reed and aquatic vegetation cover. STATUS Within the region, found only on Madagascar, where it is uncommon locally. CALL A soft 'qurr-qurr' and various frog-like croaks.

2 SAKALAVA RAIL
Amaurornis olivieri ■ 19 cm

A small, brownish-black rail with a bright-yellow bill, a red eye and reddish legs. In flight it shows dark plumage and red legs extending beyond the tail. Juv. differs from ad. in its dark-brown plumage and black bill. HABITAT Wetlands with indigenous floating vegetation; near sea level. STATUS Endemic to Madagascar; known from three sites in the west, where it is rare. CALL Unknown.

3 LESSER GALLINULE
Porphyrula alleni ■ 26–30 cm

Can be confused only with Purple Gallinule and Common Moorhen. Differs from former in its smaller size and its blue (not red) forehead. Juv. distinguished from juv. Common Moorhen by its overall paler colour, the scalloped pattern on its back and the lack of conspicuous white undertail coverts and white markings on flanks. HABITAT Freshwater areas with ample reed beds and aquatic vegetation. STATUS Uncommon throughout Madagascar; absent at higher elevations, rare in dry south. Vagrant to Comoros. CALL Six or more rapid, sharp, clicking 'duk duks'.

4 PURPLE GALLINULE
Porphyrio porphyrio ■ 38–46 cm

This huge rail, with its overall deep-blue and green coloration and bright-red bill, forehead and legs, is unmistakeable. Juv. is a duller version of ad. Not as shy as other rails, frequently venturing from cover. HABITAT Freshwater and brackish wetlands with ample reed beds and aquatic vegetation. STATUS Locally common on Madagascar but absent from higher elevations and rare in the dry south. CALL A variety of shrieks, wails and booming notes.

5 COMMON MOORHEN
Gallinula chloropus ■ 30–36 cm

Differs from the bright, glossy Lesser Gallinule mainly in its dull sooty-black plumage, distinctive white stripes on flanks and yellow-tipped red bill. Juv. similar to juv. Lesser Gallinule but is darker overall and has conspicuous white undertail coverts and white striping on flanks. Often seen swimming with unusual jerky head movements and flicking of tail. HABITAT Freshwater and brackish wetlands with reed beds surrounded by shrubby cover. STATUS Common on most islands in the region. CALL A sharp 'krrik'.

6 RED-KNOBBED COOT
Fulica cristata ■ 41–46 cm

This sooty-black, duck-like species, with its white bill and forehead, is unlikely to be confused with any of the region's other birds. Red knobs on top of white shield are engorged only during the breeding cycle. Juv. is a paler and greyer version of ad. and lacks white bill and forehead. Often seen in large flocks when not breeding. The birds dash and chase each other energetically during display. In flight, the large feet project beyond end of tail. HABITAT Freshwater and brackish wetlands with some surrounding aquatic vegetation. STATUS Uncommon on Madagascar. CALL A harsh metallic 'clack'.

1 GREATER PAINTED SNIPE   *Rostratula benghalensis* ■ 23–26 cm
In the region, can be confused only with Madagascar Snipe but is more rotund, with shorter bill and an distinctive breast pattern. Male is duller and smaller than female. HABITAT Freshwater and brackish wetlands. STATUS Within region found only on Madagascar, where it is uncommon. CALL Male utters a trill, given at dusk and at night, female answering with a soft, two-note 'wuk-oooo'.

2 MADAGASCAR SNIPE   *Gallinago macrodactyla* ■ 26 cm
This bird's very long, straight bill and striped head distinguish it from all other wetland species. Fast, zigzagging flight pattern. Juv. similar to ad. HABITAT Marshes and flooded areas, including rice paddies. STATUS Endemic to Madagascar; distributed and common in the east and north-west. CALL A noisy species during the breeding season, when it makes a drumming sound, by vibrating its stiffened outer tail-feathers, in its aerial courtship display.

3 MADAGASCAR JACANA   *Actophilornis albinucha* ■ 30 cm
An elegant, rufous bird with a black and white neck, and pale-grey frontal shield. The extremely long toes and nails, which enable it to walk over floating vegetation, are highly visible features. Juv. differs from ad. in its light-brown upperparts, whitish underparts, black cap, black back to the neck, and white sides and front of the neck. HABITAT Marshes, lakes, and ponds covered with floating vegetation. STATUS Endemic to Madagascar; distributed mostly in the west of the island (common), and locally in the east (rare). CALL A noisy species, uttering a sharp, ringing, nervous, rasping 'krrrrrrrr' reminiscent of a Dabchick (p. 32).

4 MADAGASCAR PRATINCOLE   *Glareola ocularis* ■ 25 cm
On the ground, this bird is reminiscent of a large, long-winged plover (though it sits lower than the latter) with brownish plumage, a white line on the face and a partially red bill. In flight, though, it is tern-like, with a brown breast, rufous belly and flanks, white undertail coverts and partially rufous underwing coverts. Juv. differs from ad. mainly in its upperparts which are edged with tan, streaked chest and the absence of the white face-line. HABITAT Lakes, large rivers, estuaries, rocky seashore and offshore rocky islets. STATUS Breeding endemic to Madagascar; migrant to East Africa. CALL Noisy during the breeding season, uttering a nervous, plover-like 'veet-veet-veet', most often in flight.

5 RUFF   *Philomachus pugnax* ■ m=28–30 cm f=22–26 cm
The scalloping (or scaling) on the upperparts clearly distinguishes this species from other shorebirds. Female and juv. show varying degrees of rich buff on the underparts. Some ad. males show all-white head and underparts. In flight the two distinct white oval patches on the side of the rump are diagnostic. HABITAT Fresh- and saltwater wetlands and (its preference) flooded grassy areas. STATUS Rare summer vagrant to all island groups. CALL Usually silent.

6 RUDDY TURNSTONE   *Arenaria interpres* ■ 21–24 cm
A small, stocky species with orange legs and a very short, slightly upturned bill. Br. plumage is rich mixture of bright chestnut and black upperparts with black and white head pattern. Non-br. birds drabber but with black breast-pattern and flight pattern of white wingbar and white stripes down back. HABITAT Rocky shoreline, estuaries and, infrequently, inland wetlands. STATUS Very common summer visitor to the region. CALL A hard, rattled 'kttuck' flight call.

ad.

juv.

br.

non-br.

non-br.

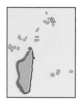

1 BLACK-WINGED STILT   *Himantopus himantopus* ■ 35–40 cm
Unlikely to be confused with any other shorebird; rendered unmistakeable by the extra-long pinkish legs and black and white plumage. Juv. has duller legs and brown (not black) upperparts and dusky nape and hind neck. In flight the black wings (upper and under) contrast with white body, and the legs trail well beyond the tail. HABITAT Various wetlands, from estuaries to inland waterbodies and large rivers. STATUS Within the region found on Madagascar, where it is fairly common except at higher elevations; vagrant to the Seychelles group. CALL A short, metallic 'kik kik' alarm note.

2 CRAB PLOVER   *Dromas ardeola* ■ 38–41 cm
This long-legged, black and white species, with its massive black bill, cannot be confused with any of the region's other shorebirds. Juv. has less well-developed bill and is grey and white with greyish wash across nape and back of neck. In flight shows very obvious black saddle and black wing-tips, with legs projecting beyond tail. HABITAT Strictly coastal, on estuaries, mangroves, tidal mudbanks and coral islands. STATUS Locally common summer visitor to all island groups. A few birds overwinter in the area. CALL Various, including a metallic 'kwa da dak' to a 'kwa da' flight call.

3 PACIFIC GOLDEN PLOVER   *Pluvialis fulva* ■ 23–26 cm
Within the region, and in non-br. plumage, can be confused only with Grey Plover, from which it differs mainly in the absence of the black 'armpits' characteristic of that species, and in its dark (not white) rump. It is also smaller and more slender, and has yellowish or buff speckling on the mantle. In flight shows a faint wingbar and uniformly grey underwings. Br. plumage shows bright golden-spangled upperparts contrasting with black underparts. HABITAT Mostly coastal, on estuaries, but also inland waterbodies. STATUS Rare summer visitor to the region; most often found in the Seychelles; rarely on Madagascar. CALL Usually a distinctive single- or two-note plaintive 'oodle-ooo' whistle.

4 GREY PLOVER   *Pluvialis squatarola* ■ 28–31 cm
Differs from somewhat similar Pacific Golden Plover in its much greyer coloration, larger size, more robust appearance and, in flight, its obvious wingbar and white (not dark) rump and diagnostic black 'armpits'. In br. plumage has black, white spangled back with black underparts and, in flight, imparts a frosty black and white appearance. HABITAT Coastal beaches, estuaries and lagoons; rarely on inland waterbodies. STATUS Common summer visitor to all island groups; a few birds overwinter. CALL A clear, plaintive 'tluuee' whistle.

ad.

juv.

1

ad.

1

ad.

2

ad.

2

juv.

ad.

non-br.

3

br.

3

non-br.

4

br.

4

non-br.

non-br.

1 LITTLE RINGED PLOVER   *Charadrius dubius* ■ 14–15 cm
In the region, can be confused with Common Ringed Plover, from which non-br. bird differs in its dark bill, yellow eye-ring and absence of wingbar. In non-br. and juv. plumage has less well-marked head, shows faint eye-ring and lacks wingbar. HABITAT Estuaries and freshwater wetlands. STATUS Summer vagrant to Seychelles. CALL Utters short, sharp 'keeuu' when flushed.

2 COMMON RINGED PLOVER   *Charadrius hiaticula* ■ 18–20 cm
In non-breeding plumage can be confused with Greater and Lesser sandplovers (p. 86) and Madagascar and Kittlitz's plovers. Easily distinguished from them all by its pinkish or orange-yellow legs and feet. Non-br. and juv. plumage bird has black, incomplete breast-band and flesh-coloured or orange legs. In flight shows white wingbar and white collar. HABITAT Mostly coastal, on estuaries and salt pans. STATUS Common summer visitor to all island groups. CALL A fluty 'tooee' and a rolling trill.

3 MADAGASCAR PLOVER   *Charadrius thoracicus* ■ 13–14 cm
Diagnostic features distinguishing this species from Kittlitz's Plover include the black forehead-line, which extends behind the eye, and the black breast-band. Distinguished from the Common Ringed Plover by smaller size, black bill, black legs and orange-washed underparts. In flight it shows a thin, white wingbar and dark tail. Juv. differs from ad. mainly in its less scaly upperparts and very pale head. HABITAT Short-grassed vegetation in coastal areas, surrounds of freshwater and brackish lakes; occasionally estuaries, mangrove stands and mudflats. STATUS Rare endemic to Madagascar, where distributed along the west and south coasts. CALL A short 'peet-peerts' trill.

4 KITTLITZ'S PLOVER   *Charadrius pecuarius* ■ 12–15 cm
Adult very similar to Madagascar Plover but is somewhat smaller and darker, and lacks that species' broad black breast-band. Juv. could be confused with Greater and Lesser sandplovers (p. 86) but is smaller, with a neater and smaller bill and a white collar. HABITAT Both fresh- and saltwater wetlands, favouring sandy or short-grassed areas. STATUS Within the region, found only on Madagascar, where it is a locally common breeder. CALL A short, clipped 'kittip'.

5 WHITE-FRONTED PLOVER   *Charadrius marginatus* ■ 14–17 cm
Smaller and paler than both Greater and Lesser sandplovers (p. 86), with a smaller bill and an obvious white hind collar. Differs from juv. Kittlitz's Plover in its paler coloration below and lack of head markings except for narrow black bar on forehead. HABITAT Mostly coastal, on beaches, lagoons, salt pans, estuaries; large rivers. STATUS Common breeding resident of Madagascar; recorded from Comoros. CALL A clear 'wiiit' note and 'tukut' alarm call.

6 THREE-BANDED PLOVER   *Charadrius tricollaris* ■ 16–18 cm
Unmistakeable shorebird with conspicuous double black breast-band. Not to be confused with br. Common Ringed and Madagascar plovers, which have a single black breast-band. At close range the grey face, red eye-ring and dark-tipped red bill are diagnostic. HABITAT Mostly freshwater areas, occasionally saltwater lagoons. STATUS Common mostly in the north and west of Madagascar; rarer elsewhere. CALL A penetrating, high-pitched 'weet weeet' whistle.

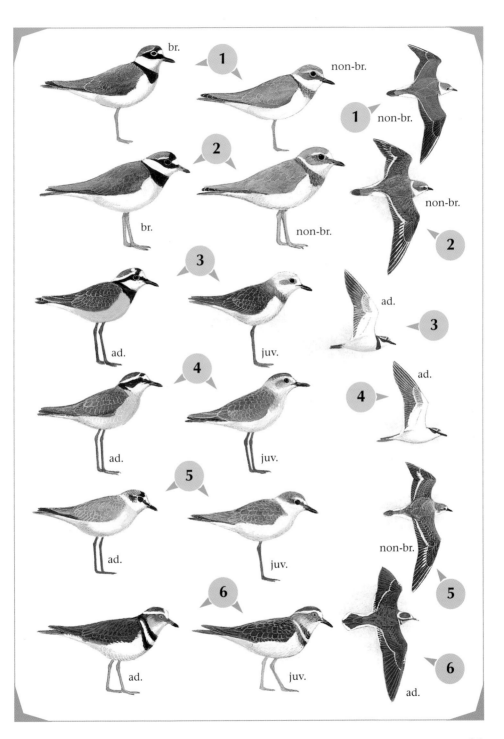

br.

1

non-br.

1 non-br.

2

br.

non-br.

non-br.

2

3

ad.

juv.

ad.

3

4

ad.

juv.

ad.

4

5

ad.

juv.

non-br.

5

6

ad.

juv.

6

ad.

1 BLACK-TAILED GODWIT
Limosa limosa ■ 40 cm

Can be confused only with Bar-tailed Godwit but is larger and more robust, and has longer legs. The broad black tip to tail and broad white wingbar, both of which are evident only in flight, are diagnostic. Bar-tailed Godwit has a barred tail and no white wingbar. At rest the Black-tailed Godwit has less mottled upperparts and a broader (at base), straighter, pink-based bill. Juv. is much buffier in appearance than ad. The head and body take on a bright rusty colour in br. plumage. HABITAT Coastal wetlands, especially tidal mudflats. STATUS Rare summer visitor to Madagascar, Comoros and Seychelles. CALL Usually silent but utters a 'weeka weeka' in flight.

2 BAR-TAILED GODWIT
Limosa lapponica ■ 38 cm

Smaller and more slender in shape than very similar Black-tailed Godwit, with shorter legs and a noticeably thinner, upturned, pink-based bill. In flight shows no obvious white wingbar (as in Black-tailed Godwit) and has a finely barred (not black-tipped) tail. The back is browner and very much more mottled and flecked, quite unlike the uniform greyish brown of the Black-tailed Godwit. In br. plumage has more extensive brick-red underparts than Bar-tailed. HABITAT Coastal wetlands and, especially, large expanses of tidal mudflats. STATUS Common summer visitor to most island groups, especially Madagascar. Vagrant to Comoros. CALL In flight utters a 'wik wik' or 'kirrrik'.

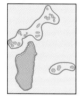

3 WHIMBREL
Numenius phaeopus ■ 40–43 cm

Differs from both godwits in its long, decurved bill. Similar to Eurasian Curlew but is much smaller, overall darker in appearance, and has a shorter decurved bill. The diagnostic black crown-stripes are easily seen at close range. In flight appears very much darker overall than Eurasian Curlew and has a faster wing-beat. HABITAT Occurs on coastal estuaries, beaches, mudflats and among mangrove stands. STATUS Common summer visitor to all island groups; some birds overwinter in the region. CALL A frequently uttered, evenly pitched, bubbling call of about seven notes.

4 EURASIAN CURLEW
Numenius arquata ■ 53–59 cm

The largest of the region's shorebirds and can be confused only with Whimbrel. Differs mainly in its larger size, longer legs, very much paler overall colour and very obvious, extra-long decurved bill. Lacks the black crown stripes of Whimbrel and, in flight, shows very white underwings, generally imparting a much paler impression than the Whimbrel. HABITAT Coastal estuaries, mudflats, mangroves and salt pans. STATUS Uncommon and infrequent summer visitor to all the region's island groups; much rarer than the abundant Whimbrel. CALL A clear, far-carrying 'curl eee'.

5 COMMON GREENSHANK
Tringa nebularia ■ 30–35 cm

Very much smaller than both godwits; most easily confused with Marsh Sandpiper (p. 84). Differs from latter in its larger size, more robust build, larger and more angled head, and thick-based, slightly upturned bill. Sometimes feeds in shallow water, pursuing prey with swift runs and side-swiping of bill. HABITAT Both freshwater and coastal wetlands. STATUS Common summer visitor to most islands in the region, with a few birds remaining throughout the year. CALL A loud and sometimes rasping 'chew chew chew' whistle.

br.

non-br.

non-br.

1

non-br.

1

br.

ad. non-br.

non-br.

2

2

non-br.

non-br.

3

4

5

1 MARSH SANDPIPER   *Tringa stagnatilis* ■ 23 cm

Most easily confused with Common Greenshank (p. 82) but is smaller, much slimmer and overall very much paler, especially on head and breast. The main difference is its very thin and straight black bill, as opposed to the robust upturned bill of Common Greenshank. In flight much more rapid, with jinky twists and a less direct line of flight than Greenshank. HABITAT Both freshwater and coastal wetlands. STATUS Uncommon summer visitor to most island groups. CALL A high-pitched, clipped 'yeup'.

2 WOOD SANDPIPER   *Tringa glareola* ■ 20 cm

Slightly smaller, more slender and overall much paler than Ruff (p. 76). Back colour dark with pale speckling over mantle and wing coverts, and lacks the female Ruff's scaly pattern. In flight has less contrasting dark back and white rump, and black underwings with white body. HABITAT Freshwater wetlands; less so brackish wetlands. Occurs in open marshy areas. STATUS Rare summer visitor to all island groups; recorded most frequently on the Comoros. CALL A piercing 'chif if if' whistle.

3 TEREK SANDPIPER   *Xenus cinereus* ■ 23 cm

This small, short-legged, stocky wader, with its long upturned bill, is unmistakeable. Legs and feet are yellow and bill has a yellow base. In flight shows a white trailing edge to wing. Runs swiftly after prey with head held low and bill pointing forward. HABITAT Mostly tidal mudflats, estuaries and salt pans; rarely on inland freshwater bodies. STATUS Common summer visitor to Madagascar; also regular visitor to the other island groups. CALL A series of fluty, uniformly pitched 'weet weet weet' notes.

4 COMMON SANDPIPER   *Actitis hypoleucos* ■ 19 cm

A small, short-legged and short-billed shorebird with a curious habit of teetering, or bobbing, backwards and forwards with a rocking motion. Differs from other similar shorebirds in its fairly uniform greyish upperparts and the clearly seen white shoulder in front of closed wing. Flight action peculiar, comprising series of quick, shallow wingbeats on bowed wings interspersed with glides. HABITAT Found in wide variety of fresh- and saltwater wetlands. STATUS Common summer visitor to virtually all islands in the region, with a few individuals overwintering. CALL A shrill, high-pitched 'titititi'.

non-br.

br.

1

2

3

4

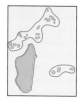

1 GREATER SANDPLOVER
Charadrius leschenaultii ∎ 22–25 cm

This and Lesser Sandplover are very similar and pose an identification problem. The Greater Sandplover is larger (only useful when both seen together) and has a longer, thicker and more robust bill. Much larger than White-fronted and juv. Kittlitz's plovers (p. 80), and lacks their white or pale hind collars. HABITAT Tidal mudflats, sandy beaches, mangroves and coastal lagoons and lakes. STATUS Common summer visitor to most of the region's larger islands. CALL Mostly silent, but sometimes utters a short, musical trill.

2 LESSER SANDPLOVER
Charadrius mongolus ∎ 19–21 cm

Easily confused with Greater Sandplover unless seen together and directly compared. Differs in its smaller size, shorter legs and smaller, neater bill with a less bulbous tip. In br. plumage has much more rufous across the breast and belly. HABITAT Tidal mudflats, mangroves, salt pans and coastal lagoons. STATUS Regular summer visitor to Seychelles; rare summer visitor to Madagascar and Comoros. CALL A harsh, Turnstone-like rattled 'chittick'.

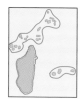

3 CASPIAN PLOVER
Charadrius asiaticus ∎ 18–22 cm

In its breeding plumage, the bird is most likely to be confused with Greater and Lesser sandplovers, but differs from them in the black border to its chestnut breast-band. In non-br. plumage differs from them in its overall slimmer appearance, longer legs, thinner and much weaker bill, complete brown breast-band and overall browner, less grey, coloration. HABITAT Most often seen in short-grassed areas but also at estuaries. STATUS Summer vagrant to Seychelles. CALL A clear 'tooeet' whistle.

4 SANDERLING
Calidris alba ∎ 20 cm

A small, very pale shorebird which differs from the smaller Little Stint by its more pallid appearance, thicker and shorter bill and, in flight, by the broad white wingbar. Superficially resembles White-fronted Plover (p. 80), which is found on the same sandy beaches but has a longer, thicker bill and and entirely different shape and feeding action. Dashes after receding waves on open shoreline to probe the wet sand. HABITAT Has preference for sandy beaches; also coastal estuaries, lagoons, mudflats. STATUS Common summer visitor to most of the region's larger islands. CALL A single, sharp 'wick' note, most often given in flight.

5 LITTLE STINT
Calidris minuta ∎ 13–15 cm

The region's smallest shorebird; can be confused only with the larger and much paler Sanderling. Smaller than Curlew Sandpiper, with a short, straight (not long, decurved) bill and, in flight, a dark (not white) rump. Feeds in frenzied fashion, with rapid 'sewing machine' stabs into mud. HABITAT Coastal salt- and freshwater wetlands. STATUS Uncommon summer visitor to most islands; vagrant to Comoros. CALL A short and sharp 'schitt'.

6 CURLEW SANDPIPER
Calidris ferruginea ∎ 18–23 cm

A grey and white wader and the region's only small shorebird with a long decurved bill, which is black. In flight has an obvious square white rump. In br. plumage the underparts are deep rufous in colour, and the white rump becomes speckled. HABITAT Coastal wetlands; occasionally inland waterbodies. STATUS Common summer visitor to most of those large islands in the region that offer suitable habitat. CALL A short 'chirrup' trill.

br.

non-br.

non-br.

br.

non-br.

non-br.

br.

non-br.

non-br.

br.

non-br.

non-br.

br.

non-br.

non-br.

br.

non-br.

non-br.

1 SUBANTARCTIC SKUA
Catharacta antarctica ■ 60–65 cm

A large brown gull-like seabird with conspicuous white crescent-shaped flashes at base of primaries. Juv. and imm. birds are much darker than ad., appearing overall dark chocolate brown with reduced white wing-flashes. Ad. is paler on head and, at close range, has pale-buff hackles on neck and even paler underparts. Much larger, broader-winged than both Pomarine and Arctic skuas. HABITAT Open seas; sometimes inshore close to islands. STATUS Regular winter visitor to the region, with some birds oversummering. CALL Silent at sea, but when alarmed or feeding will utter a 'wek wek' or 'yap yap'.

2 ARCTIC SKUA
Stercorarius parasiticus
■ 42–46 cm (12 cm more with central tail feathers)

Pale, dark and intermediate forms occur. Much slighter in build than Pomarine Skua, with narrower wing-base and pointed (not blunt-ended) tail projections. Differs from Long-tailed Skua in its larger size, bulkier build, broader wings and much shorter tail projection (if present). Juv. closely resembles juv. Long-tailed Skua but is larger and stockier in build, and has more white at primary base. HABITAT Open seas; sheltered bays during storms. STATUS Uncertain; possibly overlooked. Rare summer visitor to southern areas of the region. CALL Silent at sea.

3 POMARINE SKUA
Stercorarius pomarinus
■ 46–51 cm (25–27 cm more with central tail feathers)

This species is larger than Arctic Skua but smaller and slimmer than Subantarctic Skua. Occurs commonly in pale form, less so in dark form. The blunt-ended tail projections (when visible) are diagnostic. Shows larger white wing-patches than Arctic and Long-tailed skuas. Regularly follows flocks of Sooty Terns (p. 96), which it is often seen harrying for food. HABITAT Open seas. STATUS The region's commonest skua at sea during summer; not yet recorded from any island within the group. CALL Silent at sea.

4 LONG-TAILED SKUA
Stercorarius longicaudus
■ 38–44 cm (18 cm more with central tail feathers)

The smallest of the skuas and, if seen in br. plumage, has very long, diagnostic tail projections. With its small size and slender shape it is almost tern-like, the flight light and buoyant. Juv. and non-br. ad. show only a white shaft at primary base, lacking the white wing-patches obvious in larger skuas. HABITAT Open seas. STATUS Common in southern Mozambique Channel during summer; uncertain elsewhere in region (possibly overlooked). CALL Silent at sea.

juv. dark phase

2

2

ad. non-br. pale phase

3

juv.
dark phase

juv.

3

juv.

juv.

4

ad. non-br. pale phase

juv.

juv.

4

ad. non-br.

1 KELP GULL
Larus dominicanus ■ 55–65 cm

Can be confused only with Lesser Black-backed Gull, whose range in the region does not overlap. The only large black and white gull found on Madagascar. Juv. is dark mottled brown with pale rump, becoming paler through progressive moults until it attains the black and white ad. plumage. HABITAT Coastal beaches, ports and salt lakes. STATUS Confined to the south coast of Madagascar, where it is uncommon. Here, the bird is very different to other Kelp Gull populations and requires further taxonomic study. Birds recorded farther north in Madagascar might well be migratory Lesser Black-backed Gulls. CALL Usual gull-like yelps and a harsh 'kwok'.

2 LESSER BLACK-BACKED GULL
Larus fuscus ■ 51–61 cm

Can be confused only with Kelp Gull, but ranges are not known to overlap in the region. A large gull with black back and upper wings and, usually, bright yellow legs and feet. Juv. and imm. birds are variably mottled, becoming progressively paler with age, and in this earlier plumage have pinkish or pale flesh-coloured legs (Kelp Gull, at all ages, never shows bright yellow or pink legs and feet). HABITAT Tidal mudflats, beaches and coral islands. STATUS Irregular and uncommon summer visitor to the Seychelles. CALL Silent in the region.

3 GREY-HEADED GULL
Larus cirrocephalus ■ 41–43 cm

Within the region, the Grey-headed Gull can be confused, in non-br. and juv. plumage, only with non-br. and juv. Black-headed Gull. However, it differs in its much larger size, bulkier appearance, darker grey back, more extensive black wing-tips, dark-grey (not white) underwings and the presence of white wing 'mirrors', which Black-headed Gull lacks. Adults have pale (not dark) eyes as in ad. Black-headed Gull. Ad. in breeding plumage has obvious grey hood. HABITAT Inland freshwater lakes, where it breeds, and casually to the coast. STATUS Uncommon and localized on Madagascar; vagrant to the Comoros. CALL A typical 'karrrh', and 'pok pok' notes.

4 BLACK-HEADED GULL
Larus ridibundus ■ 37–40 cm

Smaller, neater and more compact than Grey-headed Gull and, in br. plumage, has diagnostic dark-brown hood which, from a distance, appears black. In non-br. and juv. plumage differs from similar Grey-headed Gull in its paler grey back, much more extensive white forewing and the lack of black wing-tips with white 'mirrors'. It also has a white (not grey) underwing. HABITAT Beaches, tidal mudflats and freshwater lakes and dams. STATUS Summer vagrant to Seychelles group. CALL A typical small-gull 'kraah' sound.

5 CASPIAN TERN
Hydroprogne caspia ■ 47–54 cm

The region's largest tern, easily identified by its massive red or orange-red bill. For a short period, when breeding, it has a black cap; otherwise the crown is grizzled black and white. Juv. has even less black on head, a dark-tipped bill and mottled upperparts. Could be mistaken for Swift Tern (p. 94), but its larger size and large red (not yellow bill) should rule out any confusion. HABITAT Both fresh- and salt-water wetlands. STATUS Common resident in coastal areas of Madagascar; rarer in the east and central regions. Breeds on Aldabra; vagrant to central Seychelles group and Comoros. CALL A harsh, grating 'kraaak'.

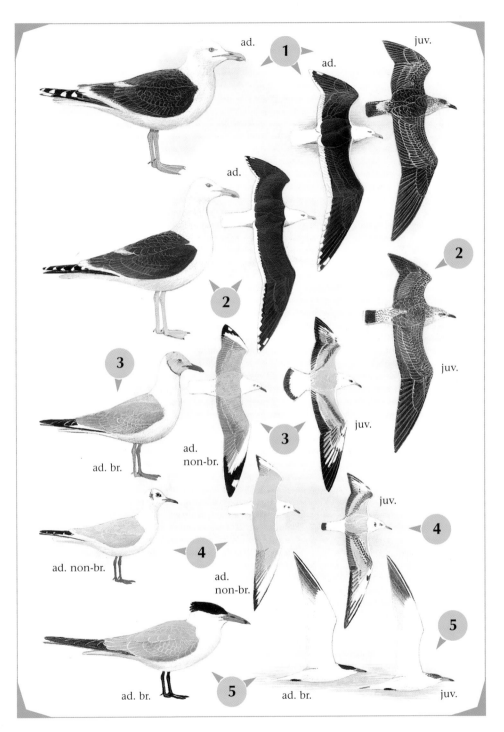

ad.

1

ad.

juv.

ad.

2

2

3

ad.
non-br.

juv.

3

ad. br.

juv.

ad. non-br.

4

4

ad.
non-br.

juv.

5

ad. br.

5

ad. br.

juv.

1 WHISKERED TERN *Chlidonias hybridus* ■ 25 cm

Within the region, can be confused only in non-br. plumage with White-winged Tern. It differs in its slightly larger size, stockier build, grey (not white) rump and the black on its head, which is confined to a dark stripe through to the nape. Flight action more powerful, with stronger wing-beats and a less dipping, buoyant motion than White-winged Tern. Never shows the black and white patterned underwing so often evident in the non-br. White-winged Tern. HABITAT Freshwater wetlands; rarely in coastal areas. STATUS Uncommon resident on Madagascar; vagrant to Seychelles and Mascarenes. CALL An often repeated and harsh 'tzzzizz', especially when breeding.

2 WHITE-WINGED TERN *Chlidonias leucopterus* ■ 23 cm

In non-br. plumage most likely to be confused with non-br. Whiskered Tern. It differs in its smaller size, daintier appearance and a dipping, buoyant flight action that involves much swooping and bill-dipping in water. The black on its head is more extensive than that of the Whiskered Tern, covering the ear coverts, and it has a white (not grey) rump. Br. plumage shows all-black body with contrasting whitish upperwing coverts. HABITAT Freshwater and brackish lakes, both coastal and inland. STATUS Rare summer visitor to Madagascar, Mascarenes and Seychelles. CALL Silent in the region.

3 COMMON TERN *Sterna hirundo* ■ 33 cm

Most likely to be confused with Roseate Tern, from which it differs in its much darker back and upperwings and shorter, forked tail. Sandwich and Gull-billed terns (p. 94) are much larger, with larger bills; non-br. Whiskered Tern has a shorter and only slightly forked tail. HABITAT Intertidal zone and offshore, roosting on sandbars and tidal mudflats. STATUS Uncertain; most probably overlooked. Recorded on all island groups as a summer visitor. CALL Sharp, clipped 'kik kik' and longer 'keee-aar' when alarmed.

4 ROSEATE TERN *Sterna dougallii* ■ 36 cm

Similar in size to Common Tern but with a much longer, deeply forked tail, much paler grey on back (in certain light conditions it appears almost white-backed) and generally has a less shaggy-naped appearance. At close range shows a distinct flush of pink over the breast, which is lacking in the Common Tern. HABITAT Intertidal zone and offshore; sandy beaches and atolls. STATUS Breeds around Madagascar and the Seychelles; recorded on Mascarenes and Comoros. Can be seen at sea throughout the region. CALL A harsh and grating 'aarrh', more like the Swift Tern (p. 94) than the smaller terns.

br.

br.

1

non-br.

non-br.

br.

br.

2

non-br.

non-br.

3

br.

br.

br.

4

br.

1 Swift (Greater Crested) Tern
Sterna bergii ■ 46–49 cm

Second in size only to Caspian Tern (p. 90), from which it differs in its thinner yellow (not massive red or orange) bill. Much larger than Lesser Crested Tern, which has an orange (not yellow) bill. In certain light conditions the yellow of the bill takes on a greenish tinge. Has unusually long, thin, graceful wings and, in flight, lacks the dark wing-tips of Caspian Tern. In br. plumage the black cap does not extend to bill base, and the head has a shaggy-crested appearance. HABITAT Coastal waters, sandy beaches, estuaries and saltwater lagoons. STATUS Breeds on many islands throughout the region; common on Madagascar and the Comoros; vagrant to Mascarenes and central Seychelles. CALL A harsh 'kreee-eck'.

2 Lesser Crested Tern
Sterna bengalensis ■ 35–38 cm

Very much smaller than the Caspian Tern (p. 90), with a much shorter and less massive, more orange bill. Most likely to be confused with Swift Tern but is smaller, with a paler back and upperwing and, as noted, an orange (not yellow) bill. In flight appears overall much paler than Swift Tern. HABITAT Coastal estuaries, offshore; roosts on rocky islets and sandbars. STATUS A summer migrant; some birds present all year. The most common tern on and around Madagascar; occurs in all of the region's other island groups. CALL A hoarse 'kreck'.

3 Gull-billed Tern
Gelochelidon nilotica ■ 35–37 cm

Very similar to Sandwich Tern but has longer legs and a much thicker-based, shorter, stubbier bill that lacks the latter's yellow tip. In non-br. and juv. plumage has very little black on head except behind the eyes and nape, and lacks the shaggy-crested look of Sandwich Tern. At rest stands higher than Sandwich Tern. In flight has a slightly forked, grey (not white, deeply forked) tail. HABITAT Coastal areas; often seen over freshwater bodies. STATUS Uncertain. Summer vagrant to Madagascar; regular visitor on Seychelles. CALL A harsh, metallic 'kek kek'.

4 Sandwich Tern
Sterna sandvicensis ■ 36–41 cm

Noticeably larger than both Common and Roseate terns (p. 92), with which it might associate, and has a diagnostic yellow-tipped bill. At a distance could be confused with Gull-billed Tern but its bill is much more slender with a slight downward droop, has much more black on the head and a more deeply forked white (not grey) tail. HABITAT Coastal; roosts on rocky islets, sandbars and mud-flats. Also open seas. STATUS Uncertain, and possibly overlooked. Vagrant to Madagascar and the Seychelles group and, at sea, to the Mozambique Channel. CALL A harsh 'krik' in flight.

5 Black-naped Tern
Sterna sumatrana ■ 30 cm

Adult could be mistaken for White Tern (p. 96) from a distance, but black nape and black outer primary feathers should rule out confusion. Juv. lacks head pattern of ad. and could be confused with non-br. Little/Saunders' Tern (p. 96) but is larger, has a longer, slightly decurved bill and lacks the dark 'wedge' to wing-tips. The breast has a pinkish tinge, which can be seen at close range and is present at all ages. HABITAT Open sea and coastal waters. Roosts on sandbars, often with other terns. STATUS Uncommon throughout the region except close to its breeding islands in the Seychelles group. CALL A clipped and repeated 'kik kik'.

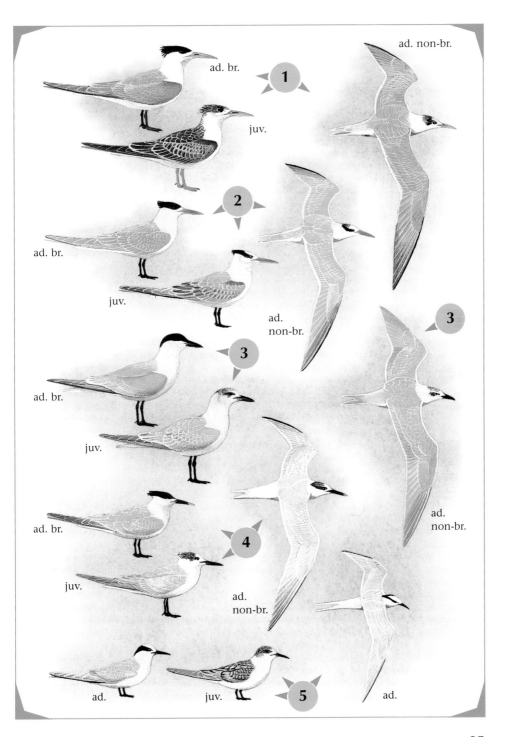

ad. non-br.

ad. br.

1

juv.

2

ad. br.

juv.

ad.
non-br.

3

3

ad. br.

juv.

ad.
non-br.

3

ad. br.

4

juv.

ad.
non-br.

ad.

juv.

5

ad.

1 COMMON (BROWN) NODDY　　　　　　　*Anous stolidus* ■ 36–45 cm
Can be confused with both Lesser Noddy and juv. Sooty Tern. Differs from former in its larger size, heavier build and thicker-based, less slender bill. It is also overall paler than Lesser Noddy, with paler underwing, and the grey on the crown does not extend beyond the nape. Differs from juv. Sooty Tern in its pale forehead and crown, and its dark (not white) vent. HABITAT Open seas, and offshore near its breeding islands. STATUS Common throughout the region, but scarce in the more southerly areas. CALL A hoarse 'kark'.

2 LESSER NODDY　　　　　　　　　　*Anous tenuirostris* ■ 30–34 cm
Differs from Common Noddy in its smaller size, more slender bill, and the grey on its head, which extends onto and merges with the brown of face and cheeks. HABITAT Open seas and inshore near breeding islands. STATUS Common to abundant near its natal islands in the Seychelles and Mascarenes; scarce at sea in the western and southern areas. CALL A short, rattling 'churrr'.

3 BRIDLED TERN　　　　　　　　　　*Sterna anaethetus* ■ 30–32 cm
Easily mistaken for Sooty Tern but has paler, brownish grey (not sooty black) upperparts, and white on forehead extending in a line to behind the eye. Juv. similar to ad. but very much paler. HABITAT Open seas, and offshore near breeding islands. STATUS Common only near its breeding islands in the Seychelles and the Mascarenes. Does not occur in large flocks. CALL A dog-like 'wup wup'.

4 SOOTY TERN　　　　　　　　　　　*Sterna fuscata* ■ 40–44 cm
Similar to but larger and very much darker on the upperparts than the Bridled Tern, the white of the forehead extending backwards only as far as the eye. Juv. could be confused with either of the two Noddy terns but the Sooty has a dark (not pale) forehead and a white (not dark) vent. HABITAT Spends most of year at sea, far from land; can be seen inshore at breeding islands. STATUS The region's most abundant tern. CALL A sharp 'wik a wik'.

5 LITTLE/SAUNDERS' TERN　　　*Sterna albifrons/saundersi* ■ 23 cm
The region's smallest tern and, because of its diminutive size, unlikely to be confused with any other species. Breeding plumage shows a small white patch on forehead and a bright dark-tipped yellow bill and yellow legs. In non-br. plumage differs from larger Black-naped Tern (p. 94) in its darker grey back and very dark-grey forewing, extending from carpals to wing-tip, which forms a black 'wedge'. HABITAT Coastal and inshore waters; rarely far out to sea. Roosts on beaches and sandbars. STATUS Common summer visitor to the Seychelles group and Madagascar. Both species recorded but almost impossible to distinguish in the field, which obscures the true status of the two (if indeed they are different species). CALL A sharp 'kik kik'.

6 WHITE (FAIRY) TERN　　　　　　　　　*Gygis alba* ■ 30 cm
Unmistakeable all-white tern. The adult Black-naped Tern (p. 94) can also appear all-white at a distance but is different in shape, with a long, forked tail and long, thin, pointed wings. At close range White Tern shows a slightly upturned black bill with a blue base, and cobalt-blue legs and feet. Juv. has a dark spot behind the eye and greyish markings on nape and mantle. HABITAT Rarely seen far from land. STATUS Locally common breeders in Seychelles; vagrant to northern Madagascar and Mascarenes. CALL A whistled alarm note; various clicks at nest.

ad.

juv.

1 MADAGASCAR SANDGROUSE
Pterocles personatus ■ 35 cm

On the ground this species, with its stout body, small head and short legs, looks rather like a pigeon. The only sandgrouse in the region, easily identified by rufous-tan plumage and black mask. In flight the silhouette appears stocky, showing broad pointed wings. Flight is swift and powerful. Generally found in small groups but often in large numbers near water sources. Female differs from male in the absence of the black mask and in its upperparts, which are tan finely striped with brown. Juv. differs from female in its smaller size and duller plumage. HABITAT Open areas such as grassland and the surrounds of lakes and rivers; from sea level to low altitude. STATUS Endemic to Madagascar; found mainly in the south and west, where it is common. CALL Vocal in flight, uttering a highly distinctive, low-pitched, nasal, repetitive 'katakataka'.

2 SPOTTED (GROUND) DOVE
Streptopelia chinensis ■ 30 cm

Small, pinkish dove with a dark back and a thick black hind-collar densely spotted with white. In flight shows a grey bar which contrasts with very dark primaries, and a longish, wedge-shaped tail with conspicuous white outertail feathers. Unlikely to be confused with the very much smaller Zebra Dove. HABITAT Agricultural lands, roadsides, and near human habitation. STATUS Introduced to Mauritius in 1781, and now common throughout the island. CALL Utters a three-noted ' coo cooo coo' call.

3 CAPE TURTLE DOVE
Streptopelia capicola ■ 28 cm

A small, greyish-brown dove which has a thin black hind-collar and, in flight, an obvious white-tipped edge to the tail. It is larger and longer-tailed than Tambourine Dove (p. 100) and lacks that species' white breast and russet wings. HABITAT Agricultural areas, roadsides and around human habitation; avoids dense forest. STATUS Introduced to Comoros; distributed on the four main islands, where locally common. CALL Utters a soft, often-repeated 'kuk cooo kuk'; a harsh 'kurr' when alarmed.

4 FERAL PIGEON
Columba livia ■ 33 cm

This species has many and varied plumages; the most common is the bluish-grey bird with a white rump, two black wingbars and, to a greater or lesser degree, a greenish oily sheen to the neck. Not likely to be confused with larger endemic pigeons on any of the islands except perhaps the Comoro Blue Pigeon (p. 100) when seen at a distance. HABITAT Never far from human settlement. STATUS Kept as pets and livestock on many islands; the feral population, descended from individuals which have escaped, is found around towns and villages. CALL A typical dove-like cooing.

5 ZEBRA (BARRED GROUND) DOVE
Geopelia striata ■ 20 cm

A tiny, slender dove with diagnostic fine black barring on the sides of breast and neck. In flight shows less white on outer tail feathers than Spotted Dove. Greyish colour of face merges into a dark-pinkish breast. HABITAT Open fields, scrub, trails and roadsides, and around human habitation. STATUS Introduced to the Seychelles and Mascarenes, where it is now common. CALL A high-pitched trilling which ends in a soft, high-pitched cooing.

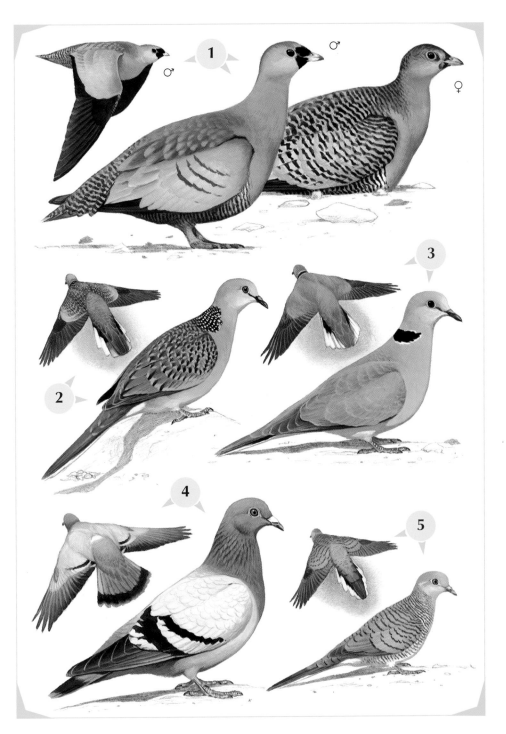

1 TAMBOURINE DOVE *Turtur tympanistria* ■ 22 cm
Unlikely to be confused with any of the region's other small doves because of its startling white face and underparts, and the chestnut wing-patches that are shown in flight. At rest it appears as a small, rotund bird with a very short tail, sharply contrasting brown upperparts and white underparts, and a white face with a very pronounced white eyebrow stripe. Juv. is greyish (not white) on underparts. Furtive and shy; most often seen as it flies from one wooded area to another. HABITAT Densely wooded gullies, gardens and patches of natural forest. STATUS Introduced to Comoros, where it is locally common on the four main islands. CALL A series of 'doo doo doo' notes.

2 NAMAQUA DOVE *Oena capensis* ■ 28 cm (including long tail)
Unmistakeable small dove with a long pointed tail and a black mask and bib. Female and juv. lack the black face and breast but still have a longish tail and, in flight, chestnut wing-patches. Very parakeet-like at rest and in flight. Flight is fast and direct. HABITAT Dry areas of Madagascar; avoids heavy rainfall regions and dense forests. STATUS Within region, occurs only on Madagascar and is locally common. CALL A distinctive, long, low-pitched hooting noise.

3 MADAGASCAR BLUE PIGEON *Alectroenas madagascariensis* ■ 28 cm
Medium-sized, dark-blue arboreal pigeon. In flight, the dark wings, without wingbars, and the blood-red tail are diagnostic. The flight is swift and powerful. Often observed in small groups perched on the top of dead tree limbs or emerging from forest canopy. Not a terrestrial species. When feeding in fruiting trees, may roost for long periods. Juv. differs from ad. in the absence of grey on breast and nape, in its dull red tail and in the small area of bare skin around its eye. HABITAT Rain forest and surrounding wooded areas; from sea level to high altitude. STATUS Endemic to Madagascar; distributed in the east and north-west, where common, making occasional seasonal incursions to the west. CALL A relatively quiet species that utters a series of liquid 'weeloo-weeloo-weeloo' whistles.

4 SEYCHELLES BLUE PIGEON *Alectroenas pulcherrima* ■ 30 cm
A large blue and white pigeon found only in the central islands of the Seychelles group. With its white head and breast and the remainder of its plumage a deep blue, it is unmistakeable. At a distance the blue appears black, but close to shows a reddish tinge. The crown is an unfeathered bright scarlet with varying degrees of wattles and wrinkles. The long white neck hackles are tipped red. HABITAT Wooded areas and fruiting trees. STATUS Confined and endemic to central Seychelles, where it is locally common. CALL A deep, hoarse cooing.

5 COMORO BLUE PIGEON *Alectroenas sganzini* ■ 30 cm
Cannot be confused with the Seychelles Blue Pigeon as the two species do not overlap. The Comoro Blue Pigeon does not have the bright scarlet crown of the Seychelles birds but does show an oval patch of bright red around the eyes. In flight, the contrasting dark body and white head and breast impart a general impression of black and white, which may just lead to confusion with the tiny brown and white Tambourine Dove. HABITAT Wooded areas; also gardens and parks. Gathers in large numbers on fruiting trees. STATUS Confined and endemic to Comoro (found on the four main islands) and Aldabra islands, where it is locally common. CALL A hoarse, almost cough-like cooing.

ad.

ad.

ad. ♂

2

ad. ♂

1

juv.

1

2

ad. ♀

3

4

5

1 COMORO OLIVE PIGEON

Columba polleni ■ 40–42 cm

The largest pigeon to be seen on the Comoro Islands and unlikely to be confused with any other species. Feral Pigeon (p. 98) is smaller, lacks the yellow bill and feet and is unlikely to be found in the same forest environment. HABITAT Forest and forest edge at higher altitudes; frequently seen at lower altitudes on suitable fruiting trees. STATUS Uncommon endemic to the Comoros, but gathers in large flocks at fruiting bushes and trees. CALL A low-pitched, raucous cooing.

2 MADAGASCAR GREEN PIGEON

Treron australis ■ 32 cm

In flight, diagnostic features are the greyish-yellow plumage below, grey-green upperparts and, especially, grey-green head, and green wings, the latter marked black with pale-yellow wingbars, and the dark-grey tail with a pale-grey terminal band. Juv. differs from ad. in its duller plumage. HABITAT Rain forest, deciduous dry forest, spiny bush forest, gallery forest, degraded woodlands; from sea level to low altitude. STATUS Endemic to Madagascar; common except in south, where uncommon. CALL A series of liquid, soft, melodious 'threeloo-threeloo-threeloo' whistles.

3 COMORO GREEN PIGEON

Treron griveaudi ■ 26–28 cm

The only green pigeon found on the Comoros and confined to the island of Mohéli. Most closely resembles Madagascar Green Pigeon but is smaller, overall very much greyer, and is especially yellower on the underparts. HABITAT Forested and wooded slopes, notably near fruiting trees. STATUS Endemic to Mohéli; uncommon. CALL Similar to Madagascar Green Pigeon but higher pitched and uttered in more rapid sequences.

4 MADAGASCAR TURTLE DOVE

Streptopelia picturata ■ 28 cm

A medium-sized brown dove with a grey head and a deep-maroon breast. Flight swift and powerful. Juv. differs from ad. in its dull, greyish-brown plumage and underparts edged with rufous. HABITAT All natural forest types, including heavily disturbed habitat; from sea level to high altitude. STATUS Originally endemic to Madagascar; probably introduced to all the other island groups. CALL Vocal, uttering a distinctive, soft, repetitive 'dae-woo dae-woo dae-woo' song.

5 SEYCHELLES TURTLE DOVE

Streptopelia picturata rostrata
and *S. p. coppingeri* ■ 26–28 cm

Has interbred with the Madagascar Turtle Dove to the extent that the Seychelles doves might not have survived in their true form. Turtle doves on Aldabra and Cosmolédo (*coppingeri*) and on a few small islands in the central Seychelles (*rostrata*) are, however, noticeably smaller and very much darker than the Madagascar Turtle Dove. They further differ in their reddish-brown (not grey) heads, chestnut (not deep reddish-brown) mantles and dark (not white) vents and lower bellies. HABITAT The species can be seen mostly on the ground, under wooded cover, and along roadsides and trails. STATUS Uncertain due to hybridization. CALL A dove-like 'droo-ooo', often repeated.

6 PINK PIGEON

Nesoenas mayeri ■ 36 cm

This very large pigeon is unmistakeable when seen both at rest and in flight. Much larger than Zebra and Spotted doves (p. 98). Juv. is duller version of ad. and darker on the head and neck. HABITAT Natural forests. STATUS Endangered Mauritian endemic, confined to remnant forest patches in the south-west of the island. CALL A deep, resonant 'hoom hoom'.

1 GREY-HEADED LOVEBIRD
Agapornis cana ■ 15 cm

This bird, with its light-grey head, throat and breast contrasting with its green body, is unmistakeable. Flight is rapid and direct, clearly revealing a green tail with a black terminal bar. Female differs from male in its green head, throat and breast. Juv. similar to female. HABITAT All forest types and sparsely wooded areas. STATUS Endemic to Madagascar; common. Introduced to the Comores, where it is common on the four main islands. CALL A high-pitched shrieking 'plee-plee-plee'.

2 GREATER VASA PARROT
Coracopsis vasa ■ 50 cm

A very large parrot with greyish brown plumage and a thick, pale bill. Distinguished from the Lesser Vasa Parrot by its larger size, stouter pale bill and the large area of bare skin around its eye. Flight is graceful, with slow wing-flapping, the pale underwing coverts contrasting with dark flight feathers. The pale undertail coverts are diagnostic. Often seen in small groups. Juv. differs from ad. in its duller brown plumage and dark bill. HABITAT All original forest types and sparsely wooded areas; from sea level to low altitude. STATUS Endemic to the region; commonly found on Madagascar and Comoros islands (except Mayotte). CALL A melodious, repeated 'pee-oo' whistle, and a raucous 'kraash-kraash' emitted when taking off or flying.

3 LESSER VASA PARROT
Coracopsis nigra ■ 35 cm

A large parrot with greyish-brown plumage. Distinguished from Greater Vasa Parrot by its smaller size, smaller bill and the reduced area of bare skin around the eye. Flight is graceful, but with faster wing-beats than Greater Vasa Parrot. Gregarious, often seen in noisy groups. Juv. differs from ad. in its duller brown plumage and dark bill. HABITAT All forest types and sparsely wooded areas; from sea level to high altitude. STATUS Endemic to the region; found on Madagascar (common), Grande Comore (common) and Anjouan (uncommon). CALL A melodious, trisyllabic 'tee-woo-tee' and, when taking off, a raucous 'kraash-kraash'.

4 SEYCHELLES BLACK PARROT
Coracopsis barklyi ■ 30–32 cm

A medium-sized parrot with greyish-brown plumage. Flight is graceful, the silhouette appearing slender, the wings long and pointed, the tail long. Juv. differs from ad. in its duller brown plumage and dark bill. HABITAT Forest; from sea level to low altitude. STATUS Endemic to the Seychelles; found only on Praslin and Curieuse, where it is common. CALL A high-pitched, melodious, often-repeated whistle when perched or in flight, and a raucous 'kraash-kraash' when taking off.

5 MAURITIUS (ECHO) PARAKEET
Psittacula echo ■ 36 cm (including long tail)

Very similar to Ring-necked Parakeet, and best distinguished by its call. Female has an all-dark bill, the male a coral-red bill. HABITAT Found only in the last remnant patches of native forest of the Black River valley in southern Mauritius. STATUS Endemic to Mauritius, where extremely rare. CALL A loud 'kaark kaark' in flight, and a short, sharp 'kik kik' alarm call.

6 RING-NECKED PARAKEET
Psittacula krameri ■ 35–40 cm

Can be confused with the endemic Mauritius Parakeet, but habitats and, most especially, calls are different. It also appears paler green with blue (not green) central feathers. HABITAT Wooded areas and agricultural lands; less so native forests. STATUS Escapees have established populations on Mauritius and Réunion; locally common. CALL High-pitched shrieks and shrills.

1 MADAGASCAR COUCAL   *Centropus toulou* ■ 45–50 cm
In its breeding plumage this coucal is shiny black with bright rufous wings; in non-br. plumage the head, neck, breast, and mantle are tan, heavily streaked and flecked with black. Flight silhouette is characteristic, with long, shiny-black tail and short, rounded, rufous wings. Often found in pairs. Male slightly smaller than female. Juv. similar to ad. in non-br. plumage. HABITAT Dense underbrush of different forest types, secondary forest, forest edge, mangrove stands, dense aquatic vegetation; from sea level to high altitude. STATUS Endemic to the region; found on Madagascar and Aldabra. On Madagascar it is distributed across the whole island, and is common; also common on Aldabra. CALL A very vocal species with a characteristically liquid, bubbling 'togoo-toogoo-toogoo-togoo', descending in scale. Individuals respond to each other's calls.

2 THICK-BILLED CUCKOO   *Pachycoccyx audeberti* ■ 34–36 cm
The adult is dark grey above and has white to buff unmarked underparts. Juv. has a clearly marked grey and white head with coverts and flight feathers tipped by large white spots. Unlikely to be confused with any of the region's other birds; all other similar-sized cuckoos have barring on the underparts. HABITAT Rain forests. STATUS Uncertain, but recently reported from the north-eastern and south-eastern parts of Madagascar, the only island in the region on which the species is found. CALL Utters a repeated, ringing 'wee-yes-yes', and a harsh 'were-wik'.

3 MADAGASCAR LESSER CUCKOO   *Cuculus rochii* ■ 28 cm
A small cuckoo with a slender silhouette, dark grey above with white underparts heavily barred with grey. Discrete; its characteristic three- or four-note call during breeding season indicates its presence. In flight, the wings appear long, narrow and sharp and the tail long. Flight is direct with rapid, rather shallow wing-beats alternating with short gliding periods. Cannot be confused with any other coua or cuckoo on Madagascar. Care must taken, however, when identifying 'grey' migrant cuckoos on other island groups. This species does not have a rufous form. Juv. similar to ad., with mottled rufous on underparts. HABITAT Different forest types, secondary forest, forest edge, mangrove, exotic tree plantations; from sea level to high altitude. STATUS A breeding endemic to Madagascar, where it occurs throughout the island during summer. Most of the population winters in eastern Africa, although some individuals are present throughout the year. CALL A very vocal species, with a characteristic call uttered both during the day, and, to a lesser degree, at night. The call comprises a three- or four-note 'kew-kew-kow' or 'kew-kew-kew-kow' sequence, the last note lower on the scale.

ad. br.

1

non-br.

2

juv.

ad.

3

juv.

ad.

1 GREEN-CAPPED COUA
Coua olivaceiceps ■ 42 cm

Very similar to Red-capped Coua, but differs in the greenish-brown top to the head and paler upperparts, wings and tail. Differs from Running Coua in its larger size and the solid-blue area of bare skin around the eye which is underlined by a thick black line. Often perches in trees to hide or when calling. HABITAT Deciduous dry forest, subarid thorn scrub, and adjacent wooded areas; from sea level to low altitude. Occurs locally alongside Red-capped Coua. STATUS Endemic to Madagascar; commonly found in the south-west and south; common in its range. CALL Similar to that of Red-capped Coua; very vocal during the breeding season.

2 RED-CAPPED COUA
Coua ruficeps ■ 42 cm

A medium-sized terrestrial coua with a slender, long-legged silhouette. Differs from the Green-capped Coua in the bright rufous top to its head and darker upperparts, wings and tail; and from Coquerel's Coua in its slimmer silhouette, rufous cap, maroon chest and the solid-blue patch of bare skin around the eye. Although ground-living, often perches in trees to hide, or when calling. Juv. differs from ad. in its brownish crown, the reduced area of bare skin around the eye and the buff-tipped feathers on its upperparts. HABITAT Deciduous dry forest and adjacent wooded areas. STATUS Endemic to Madagascar and found in the west, where it is common. CALL Utters a loud 'koa-koa-koa' mainly at dusk, and a distinctive 'yew yew yew kuh kuh kuh', the last three notes descending in scale.

3 RUNNING COUA
Coua cursor ■ 40 cm

Differs from Green-capped Coua in its slimmer build, in the tan sides of its neck and chest, and in the bare blue skin around the eye, underlined with a thinner black line. The area of bare skin is marked with a red dot. HABITAT Subarid thorn scrub close to sea level. STATUS Endemic to Madagascar; occurs in the south; uncommon. CALL A loud, clear 'kew-kew-kew-koor-koor'. Individual birds respond to each other's calls.

4 GIANT COUA
Coua gigas ■ 62 cm

A large terrestrial coua with a very long tail and stout bill. The size alone is diagnostic. Easily distinguished from similar Coquerel's Coua by its massive bulk and thick-based, powerful bill; and from the Red-capped Coua by the greenish top to its head, whitish throat and the area of bare blue skin around the eye. The bare area is marked with a large red dot. Although ground-living, often perches in a tree to hide or when calling. HABITAT Deciduous dry forest, subarid thorn scrub and gallery forest. STATUS Endemic to Madagascar; found in the west and south; common. CALL Vocal during the breeding season, uttering both a loud, guttural 'ayoo-ew' and a clear 'koo-koo-koo-koo-goo-goo'.

5 COQUEREL'S COUA
Coua coquereli ■ 42 cm

A medium-sized terrestrial coua with a colour pattern very similar to that of the Giant Coua, but noticeably smaller in size and with a thinner, less robust bill. Distinguished from Red-capped and Green-capped couas by the dark-green top to the head, rufous belly, pale throat and chest, and in the area of bare blue skin, which is marked with a red dot, around the eye. HABITAT Rain forest and deciduous dry forest; from sea level to mid altitude. STATUS Endemic to Madagascar; commonly found in the north, north-west and west. CALL Vocal during the breeding season, uttering a loud 'ayoo-ew' but higher pitched than that of the Giant Coua; and a clear 'kew-kew-kew'. Individuals respond to each other's calls.

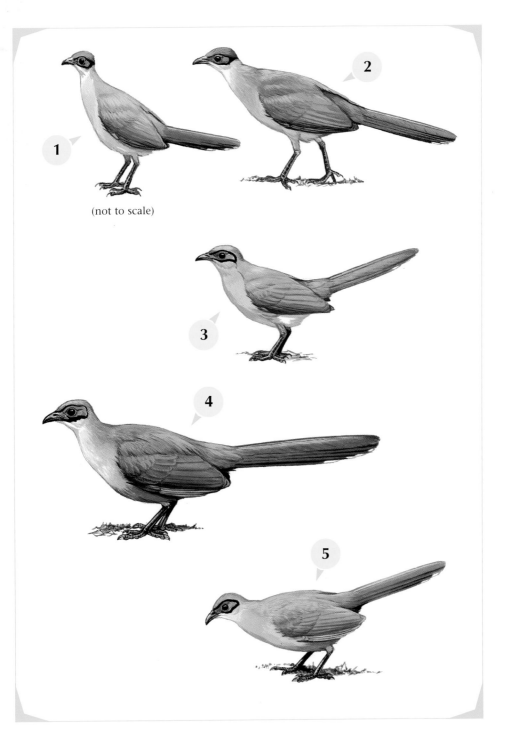

(not to scale)

1 RED-BREASTED COUA
Coua serriana ■ 42 cm

A medium-sized, long-legged, terrestrial coua with a very distinctive plumage, dark brown above and partly chestnut below. Distinguished from Red-fronted Coua by its much larger size, dark-brown crown and throat and chestnut breast. Distinguished from all other rain-forest terrestrial species by its streamlined silhouette and very long tail. HABITAT Rain forest from sea level to mid altitude. STATUS Endemic to Madagascar; commonly found in the north- and mid-east. CALL Vocal in breeding season, uttering a loud, raucous 'kooaa' repeated several times. Individuals respond to each other's calls.

2 RED-FRONTED COUA
Coua reynaudii ■ 40 cm

A small, partly terrestrial, partly arboreal coua identified by its rather short-legged silhouette, rufous forehead and solid grey underparts. Distinguished from the Red-breasted Coua, which shares the same habitat, by its much smaller size, bright rufous forehead, greenish upperparts and solid-greyish underparts. Juv. differs from ad. in its dull brown cap, reduced eye area of bare skin and the buff-tipped feathers on its upperparts. HABITAT Rain forest and secondary growth in adjacent areas; from sea level to very high altitude. STATUS Endemic to Madagascar; commonly found in the north-east, east and south-east. CALL A plaintive 'kooaa' that decreases in intensity.

3 BLUE COUA
Coua caerulea ■ 50 cm

A large arboreal coua with an unrelieved dark-blue plumage and an extensive, and distinctive, area of bare, ultramarine skin around the eye. When gliding from tree to tree, it shows a bulky silhouette with short, broad wings and long tail. Juv. differs from ad. in the much-reduced eye-patch of bare skin and its dark-brown upperparts. HABITAT Rain forest and adjacent wooded areas. STATUS Endemic to Madagascar; found in the east and north-west; common. CALL A brief, distinctive 'brreee' and a series of loud, evenly spaced 'koa-koa-koa' notes.

4 CRESTED COUA
Coua cristata ■ 42 cm

A medium-sized arboreal coua (ssp. *maxima*, found in the south-east, is much larger). The crested grey head, combined with bluish upperparts and tail and the orangey chest, are distinctive. When gliding from tree to tree it shows short, broad wings and a long, white-tipped tail. Distinguished from Verreaux's Coua in its larger size, grey chin and throat, orangy chest, rufous undertail coverts and the larger area of blue, bare skin around the eye. HABITAT Rain forest, deciduous dry forest, subarid thorn scrub, and adjacent wooded areas. STATUS Endemic to Madagascar; common in west and south; uncommon in east. CALL Utters a loud, descending 'koa-koa-koa', mainly before sunset. Individuals respond to each other's calls to create a pleasantly melodic twilight chorus.

5 VERREAUX'S COUA
Coua verreauxi ■ 38 cm

A small arboreal coua with a streamlined silhouette. The grey head and fluffy crest, the light green-grey upperparts and whitish underparts are distinctive. In its flight from tree to tree it shows short broad wings and a long white-tipped tail. Distinguished from Crested Coua by its smaller size, uniform whitish underparts lacking the rufous vent, darker-tipped crest, and smaller eye-patch of bare blue skin. HABITAT Subarid thorn scrub near sea level. STATUS Endemic to Madagascar; found in the extreme south, where uncommon. CALL A 'koy-koy-koy' repeated three or four times; higher pitched than that of the Crested Coua.

C.c. maxima

(not to scale)

1 MADAGASCAR LONG-EARED OWL   *Asio madagascariensis* ■ 40–50 cm

A large, powerful owl with tan underparts flecked with dark brown, long ear-tufts, and orange eyes. Distinguished from African Marsh Owl (p. 114) by its larger size, longer ear-tufts, and dark-brown upperparts mixed with tan. Male smaller than female. Imm. similar to ad. Nestling entirely white except for black mask and brown wings. HABITAT Rain forest, deciduous dry forest, gallery forest, and secondary forest. STATUS Endemic to Madagascar; common except in the south, where uncommon. CALL A vocal species with a characteristically loud, harsh 'Kahaan-kahaan-Kahaan' preceding a vocal 'kang-kang-kang-kang'.

2 BARN OWL   *Tyto alba* ■ 32–36 cm

This is the region's only very pale owl, differing from similar Madagascar Red Owl in its larger size, pale (not orange-red) body, and whiter underparts. Nocturnal, but does venture out to hunt at twilight. HABITAT Grasslands; open wooded areas; around human habitation. STATUS Common on Madagascar, Seychelles and Comoros. CALL Utters various sounds, the most often an eerie 'shree'.

3 MADAGASCAR RED OWL   *Tyto soumagnei* ■ 30 cm

The uniform orange colour and wide facial disk are diagnostic. Easily distinguished from Barn Owl by its smaller size, the black spots on wings, and orange facial disk. Juv. unknown. HABITAT Rain forest and adjacent secondary growth. Hides in dense foliage during day. STATUS Endemic to Madagascar; found in east and north-east; rare. CALL A hissing 'shreeee', higher pitched than Barn Owl.

4 WHITE-BROWED OWL   *Ninox superciliaris* ■ 30 cm

The heavily barred throat and chest and the large white eyebrows are typical of this medium-sized brown owl. Distinguished from the Madagascar Scops Owl (p. 114) by its larger size, plumper silhouette, dark (not yellow) eye, and absence of ear-tufts. HABITAT Deciduous dry forest, subarid thorn scrub, gallery forest; adjacent secondary forest and, in some areas, rain forest. STATUS Endemic to Madagascar; found in west, north and south (common), and locally in north-east (uncommon). CALL A 'hoo-oo-hoo-oo' preceding a 'kiang-kiang-kiang-kiang'.

5 AFRICAN MARSH OWL   *Asio capensis* ■ 32–38 cm

In its habitat the species could only be confused with the Barn Owl (p. 112), from which it differs in its overall very much darker colour, with much darker underparts. Shows buff panels on wings both in flight and at rest. The tiny ear-tufts and dark eyes are conspicuous features when seen close to. HABITAT Diverse: open fields, shrubby grasslands, marshes, reedbeds, even around human habitation. STATUS Within the region, confined to Madagascar, where it is uncommon and patchily distributed throughout the island. CALL A cricket-like 'krrik krrrik krrrik'.

1 MADAGASCAR SCOPS OWL
Otus rutilus ∎ 22–24 cm

A small owl with grey or rufous plumage, ear-tufts, and yellow eyes. Distinguished from the White-browed Owl (p. 112) by its smaller size, slimmer silhouette, flecked (not barred) underparts. The grey morph is the more common; rufous morph restricted to rain forest habitat. Rufous morph might be confused with Madagascar Red Owl (p. 112) but is smaller and has ear-tufts and yellow (not dark) eyes. HABITAT Found in most wooded areas, from sea level to high altitude. STATUS Endemic to Madagascar, and to Mayotte in the Comoros; common throughout its range. CALL Very vocal species; utters a diagnostic muffled, monotonous 'broo-broo-broo-broo-broo'.

2 SEYCHELLES SCOPS OWL
Otus insularis ∎ 20–22cm

The only small owl occurring on Mahé, largest island of the Seychelles group. The bird has only one colour phase, and its eyes are large and golden yellow. Rarely seen at roost during daylight; can be located at night by its diagnostic call. HABITAT Well forested slopes and valleys at the higher elevations. STATUS Uncommon; endemic to and found in isolated pockets on Mahé. CALL A continuous, harsh 'waugh waugh'; various 'tok tok' notes.

3 KARTHALA SCOPS OWL
Otus pauliani ∎ 20–22 cm

The only small owl found on the forested slopes of Mt. Karthala, Grande Comore; characterized by dark head, large yellow eyes and pale-buffy breast. The bird is very inquisitive: it will quickly respond to a playback of its call. HABITAT Forests and forest edge; marginally into large scrub heath. Avoids exotic plantations. STATUS Common endemic in forests on the upper slopes of Mt. Karthala. CALL A continuous whistled 'toot' given at one-second intervals.

4 ANJOUAN SCOPS OWL
Otus capnodes ∎ 20–22 cm

The only small owl found on Anjouan, Comoro Islands. Occurs in two colour phases, greyish and rufous, which are often seen together. Ear-tufts very reduced. Like the Karthala Scops Owl, the bird is very inquisitive and is often heard calling during the day. HABITAT Forests and forest edge on steep mountain slopes. STATUS Uncertain, but almost certainly a rare endemic to Anjouan, where it survives in the remaining few patches of native forest. CALL A distinct, long drawn-out whistle, repeated often and separated by short interludes.

5 COLLARED NIGHTJAR
Caprimulgus enarratus ∎ 24 cm

A large, brownish forest nightjar, distinguished from Madagascar Nightjar by its greater size and bright rufous nape. In flight shows white-tipped outer tail-feathers. Female and juv. differ from male in lacking white on tail. HABITAT Rain forest, adjacent secondary forest and, locally, deciduous dry forest. STATUS Endemic to Madagascar; found in the east, north and north-west; uncommon. CALL Unknown.

6 MADAGASCAR NIGHTJAR
Caprimulgus madagascariensis ∎ 21 cm

Distinguished from Collared Nightjar by its smaller size and absence of rufous nape. In flight, wings appear long and narrow, and are marked with white spots. Female differs from male in its duller plumage, the creamy spots on its upper-wing coverts, and in the absence of white on the tail. HABITAT Open areas, forests, parks and gardens; roosts on urban buildings. STATUS Endemic to the region and commonly found throughout Madagascar and Aldabra. CALL A distinctive 'pyok-top-top-top-top-top' uttered throughout the night.

brown phase

grey phase

1

2

3

dark phase

4

brown phase

5

6

1 ALPINE SWIFT
Apus melba ■ 22 cm

The region's largest swift and the only one with a white belly. Noticeably larger than the Madagascar Black Swift, with which it often associates, sharing the breeding cliffs. HABITAT Breeds on cliffs of mountainous areas, but wanders widely and can be seen over virtually any habitat. STATUS Within the region, confined to Madagascar, where locally common. CALL A shrill, staccato scream.

2 EUROPEAN (EURASIAN) SWIFT
Apus apus ■ 16–18 cm

Very similar to the Madagascar Black Swift, from which it can be distinguished only when seen close to and in good light, differing in its overall darker appearance and more uniform brown underparts. It also lacks markings on both the breast and belly feathers that give the Madagascar Black Swift a scaled appearance. The inner secondaries do not contrast with mantle and upperwings as in Madagascar Black Swift. HABITAT Aerial and wide-ranging; could occur above any kind of habitat. STATUS Rare summer vagrant to Seychelles, where identification of large swifts needs fuller investigation. CALL Silent in the area.

3 MADAGASCAR BLACK SWIFT
Apus balstoni ■ 16–18 cm

Not likely to be confused with any other all-dark swift in the region except perhaps the Palm Swift. It differs from that species in its much darker colouring, overall much bulkier shape and its slightly (not deeply) forked tail. Not easily told apart from European Swift but is paler and has paler inner secondaries, which contrast with mantle and upperwing. It also has scaly, mottled underparts. HABITAT Breeds on cliffs in highlands but far-ranging and can be seen over virtually any habitat. STATUS Endemic to Madagascar and the Comoros. CALL A high-pitched screaming 'sreee sreee' uttered in flight near breeding colonies.

4 LITTLE SWIFT
Apus affinis ■ 12–14 cm

A small black and white swift which might be confused with Madagascar Spine-tailed Swift but has a large white (not small inconspicuous grey) rump. HABITAT Wide ranging; prefers nesting among buildings in urban areas. STATUS Regular migrant to Madagascar; recorded once over Mahé, Seychelles. CALL A soft twittering and high-pitched screeching.

5 MADAGASCAR SPINE-TAILED SWIFT
Zoonavena grandidieri ■ 12 cm

A small, brown forest swift with rather long, narrow wings showing a light wing-bar, greyish rump and a short square tail. Distinguished from the Madagascar Black Swift by its smaller size, grey rump and short, square tail, and from the Little Swift by its brown colour and pale (not white) rump. Found in small, loose-knit groups. HABITAT Forested areas. STATUS Common endemic to Madagascar and Grande Comore. CALL A soft, high-pitched 'zreee' scream.

6 AFRICAN PALM SWIFT
Cypsiurus parvus ■ 15–17 cm

The species has an unmistakeable flight shape, its long, thin wings swept back and long, deeply forked tail held closed so as to appear pointed. Often seen in small groups flying rapidly and swooping around stands of palms, including those in towns. HABITAT Open areas, light woodland with palms, palm savanna, large clusters of palm thicket. STATUS Common in most coastal areas and lower elevations of Madagascar and Comoros; uncommon in the dry south of Madagascar. CALL A soft, high-pitched scream.

1 SEYCHELLES SWIFTLET
Collocalia elaphra ■ 10–12 cm

The only small swift occurring in the central Seychelles. Differs from vagrant Little Swift (p. 116) in its grey (not black) body and dark (not white) rump. Small groups can often be seen flying together over rocky outcrops and forested gullies and along forest road-clearings. HABITAT Wide-ranging, but most often seen near breeding caves in the mountains and foraging over lowlands. STATUS Endemic to central Seychelles. CALL A soft twittering (in flying groups); a metallic clicking (within breeding caves).

2 MASCARENE SWIFTLET
Collocalia francica ■ 10–12 cm

A small, greyish-brown swift with paler grey underparts, a pale rump and a slightly forked tail, which sometimes appears square-ended. The only swift occurring on the Mascarenes. HABITAT Wide-ranging; breeds in caves; often seen around mountain cliffs and gullies. STATUS Common endemic to Mauritius and Réunion. CALL Soft twitterings and metallic clicks uttered inside breeding caves.

3 BROWN-THROATED SAND MARTIN
Riparia paludicola ■ 12 cm

A small brown and white swallow which could be mistaken for the larger Mascarene Martin but lacks the latter's streaking on the underparts. HABITAT Wetlands of all kinds, especially those with sandy surroundings in which to nest. STATUS Within region, occurs only on Madagascar; common in east and north-west and over the higher central plateau. CALL A soft, unclear twittering.

4 MASCARENE MARTIN
Phedina borbonica ■ 14 cm

A chunky, brown swallow with short, triangular wings, slightly forked tail, whitish throat; breast, upper belly and flanks heavily striped with brown; white lower belly and undertail coverts. Distinguished from Brown-throated Sand Martin by larger size, bulkier silhouette, and heavily striped underparts. Distinguished from Mascarene Swiftlet by much wider, shorter wings, and much heavier flight. Juv. differs from ad. in the lighter fringes to the secondaries. HABITAT All original forest type; secondary forest; rocky outcrops; wetlands. STATUS Breeding endemic to Madagascar (common), Réunion and Mauritius (uncommon); vagrant to Seychelles. CALL A high-pitched 'trizzz' and melodious notes uttered in flight.

5 BARN (EUROPEAN) SWALLOW
Hirundo rustica ■ 15–18 cm

This bird, with its combination of black upperparts and pale underparts, and the brick-red throat and forehead of the adult, is unmistakeable within the region. Juv. has a whitish throat and incomplete black bar across breast. Adult plumage is an iridescent blue-black; adult male has very long outer tail-feathers which, when spread, show white spots. HABITAT Cosmopolitan. STATUS Uncommon to rare summer vagrant to Madagascar and Seychelles. CALL Silent in the region.

6 SAND MARTIN
Riparia riparia ■ 12 cm

Can be confused only with the Mascarene Martin and Brown-throated Sand Martin, but has distinctive white underparts and brown breast-band. Lacks the streaked underparts of the larger Mascarene Martin, and the uniformly brown throat and breast of Brown-throated Sand Martin. HABITAT Mainly near or above wetland areas. STATUS Species is a summer vagrant to Madagascar and Seychelles. CALL Silent in the region.

1 MADAGASCAR KINGFISHER   *Corythornis vintsioides* ■ 15 cm
Diagnostic features of this aquatic bird are its combination of electric blue upperparts and orange underparts, and its long, sharp black bill. Flight is fast and direct. The only blue kingfisher in the region. Found alone or in pairs. Juv. differs from ad. in its dull-blue upperparts and whitish underparts washed with orange. HABITAT Freshwater lakes, rivers, marshes, rice paddies; also mangrove stands, seashore and coralline islets; from sea level to mid altitude. STATUS Restricted to Madagascar and the Comoros. Madagascar: distributed throughout island; very common. Comoros: found on the four main islands; common. CALL A high-pitched 'treeeeeeee' given in flight.

2 MADAGASCAR PYGMY KINGFISHER   *Ispidina madagascariensis* ■ 14 cm
A small forest kingfisher with orange upperparts, white underparts, and a bright orange bill. Flight is fast and direct. Usually found alone. Juv. differs from ad. in the duller orange of its upperparts and bill. HABITAT Rain forest, deciduous dry forest, and gallery forest; from sea level to mid altitude. STATUS The species is endemic to Madagascar; found throughout the island; common except in the south, where it is very rare (restricted to just two sites). CALL A faint, high-pitched 'freeeeeeee' given in flight.

3 BLUE-CHEEKED BEE-EATER   *Merops persicus* ■ 23–31 cm
Can be confused only with the Madagascar Bee-eater, from which it differs mainly in its green (not brown) crown. It also has paler green upperparts and more noticeable blue eyebrow and cheek stripes. HABITAT Open grasslands, frequently near water and woodland fringes; often seen on telephone wires. STATUS Rare summer vagrant to the Seychelles. Very likely overlooked because of its similarity to Madagascar Bee-eater. CALL Silent in the area.

4 MADAGASCAR BEE-EATER   *Merops superciliosus* ■ 23–31 cm
Unmistakable bird with a slender silhouette, green plumage and fairly long, slightly decurved bill, narrow and pointed wings, and green tail with elongated central tail feathers. Gregarious, found in groups of up to several dozen individuals. Juv. differs from ad. in its duller green plumage and lack of tail streamers. HABITAT All original forest types and secondary forest, wetlands, farmland, and plantations; from sea level to high altitude. STATUS In the region, found on Madagascar and the Comoro Islands. In Madagascar, found throughout the island, where it is common. In the Comoros, found on Grande Comore, Mohéli, and Mayotte, where common, especially near the coast; rarely observed on Anjouan. Individual birds may move between Africa and Madagascar. CALL A very vocal species, uttering a rapid succession of fluted 'twooroop twooroop' notes in flight.

1
juv.
ad.

2
juv.
ad.

3
juv.
ad.

4
juv.
ad.

1 EUROPEAN ROLLER
Coracias garrulus ■ 31 cm

This species, with its blue head contrasting brilliantly with chestnut mantle, is unmistakeable. In flight, it shows bright-blue upper- and underwings that contrast with the bluish-black flight feathers. Juv. has a more olive tinge to its blue plumage. HABITAT The bird is usually found on exposed perches in drier areas; avoids deep forest and dense thickets. STATUS Summer vagrant to Seychelles. CALL Usually silent in non-breeding areas.

2 BROAD-BILLED ROLLER
Eurystomus glaucurus ■ 32 cm

This species, the region's only breeding roller, is a large, stocky, yellow-billed bird which appears dark when perched. In flight shows a blue tail and purple wing-coverts. Very aerial; distinguished in flight from the Madagascar Kestrel (p. 66) by the angled wings and deep wing-beats. Found in pairs, sometimes in loose groups. Juv. differs from ad. in its drabber plumage and dull brownish-yellow bill. HABITAT Rain forest, deciduous dry forest, gallery forest; also, locally, among rocky outcrops; from sea level to mid altitude. STATUS Summer breeding visitor to Madagascar; common throughout the island. Vagrant to the Comoros. Migrates to eastern Africa after breeding season. CALL Noisy during breeding season. Utters a loud, harsh, dissonant 'sararaka-sararaka-sararaka' when perched or in flight. Call often taken up by other individuals.

3 MADAGASCAR CUCKOO-ROLLER
Leptosomus discolor ■ 50 cm

A large arboreal bird with a distinctive, rather heavy silhouette, massive head and very short legs. Its black-capped grey head, the black band across the eye, the grey and white underparts and the metallic green shoulders, with blue sheen, are characteristic. In flight appears dark above and light below, with dark flight feathers and tail. Flight is slow, undulating, with supple, deep wing-beats. Usually found in pairs or family groups. Female differs from male in its plumage, which is uniformly brown except for pale underparts marked with large dark-brown blotches. Juv. differs from female in its duller brown plumage and faint breast-band. HABITAT Rain forest, deciduous dry forest, spiny bush forest, and adjacent degraded areas; from sea level to high altitude. STATUS Endemic to the region; found commonly throughout Madagascar, and the Comoros except Grande Comore. CALL Highly vocal, uttering a distinctively loud, liquid 'dree-oo-dree-oo-dree-oo' whistling call repeated many times in flight and at rest.

4 COMORO CUCKOO-ROLLER
Leptosomus gracilis ■ 40–45 cm

Much smaller than Madagascar Cuckoo-Roller, with a very well-defined blue-grey throat and upper breast, which ends abruptly to contrast with clear white underparts (these are more strikingly white in the female). Female is slightly smaller than male, and has much paler and less heavily spotted and blotched underparts than female Madagascar Cuckoo-Roller. HABITAT Forests and secondary growth on the slopes of Mt. Karthala, Grande Comore. STATUS Common endemic to Grande Comore. CALL Whistled display call similar to that of Madagascar Cuckoo-Roller but faster and higher pitched.

1 Scaly Ground-Roller
Brachypteracias squamiger ■ 30 cm

The species has bronze-green upperparts which contrast with whitish underparts scaled with black. Head scaly with a central black band and rufous nape; tail mostly rufous with sky-blue tip and bronze-green base. Usually seen on the ground. Looks actively for prey among leaf litter, its short runs alternating with long waiting periods. When threatened, freezes instantly and then slowly walks away. Rarely flies. Juv. differs from ad. in its faint black 'moustache'. HABITAT Undisturbed rain forest, from sea level to mid altitude. STATUS Endemic to Madagascar; found in east, where it is uncommon. CALL In breeding season, utters a throaty 'coor-coor' from the ground or a low branch.

2 Short-legged Ground-Roller
Brachypteracias leptosomus ■ 38 cm

This bird, the largest of the ground-rollers, shows bronze-green upperparts contrasting with white underparts which, except for a pure white upper breast band, are barred with brown. It has a dark-blue head with a conspicuously large white supercilium and white, fluffed-out throat. Tail brown except for white-tipped external tail feathers. Forages over leaf litter. In flight, which is direct and noisy, white tips to tail feathers very noticeable. Juv. differs from ad. in its faint breast-band. HABITAT The most humid parts of undisturbed rain forests; from sea level to mid altitude. STATUS Endemic to Madagascar; hard to locate; found in east, where uncommon. CALL Utters a deep 'coo-au' in breeding season.

3 Pitta-like Ground-Roller
Atelornis pittoides ■ 26 cm

Small bird, with bronze-green upperparts which contrast with sometimes fluffed-out white throat; bright blue head with white supercilium, black band across eye, blue breast-collar and orange nape, lower breast and flanks. Seen mostly on the ground. Juv. differs from ad. in its whitish throat speckled with brown. HABITAT Undisturbed rain forest; from sea level to mid altitude. STATUS Endemic to Madagascar. Commonly found in east; easily located by call. CALL A muffled 'boo' in breeding season. Individuals respond to each other's calls.

4 Rufous-headed Ground-Roller
Atelornis crossleyi ■ 26 cm

The smallest of the ground-rollers, with bronze-green upperparts, wings and tail, and a rufous head and belly. Black breast-collar has white streaks. Mostly seen on the ground, where it shows a plump silhouette and rather long, slender legs. Juv. differs from ad. in its faint black breast-collar. HABITAT Undisturbed rain forest, from sea level to mid altitude. STATUS Endemic to Madagascar; found in east; uncommon. CALL In breeding season, the bird utters a muffled 'boo' resembling the call of Pitta-like Ground-Roller but slightly higher pitched.

5 Long-tailed Ground-Roller
Uratelornis chimaera ■ 47–52 cm

The only ground-roller with a long tail. Upperparts are brown mottled with white; underparts white crossed by a black breast-band; contrasting head-pattern, with a dark band across the eye framed by a light white supercilium and a large white 'moustache'. Very long, brown, black-barred tail edged in sky-blue. Can be seen both on the ground and perched in trees, in each case showing its plump silhouette and very long tail, which is longer on male than on female. Juv. differs from female in the faint black bands on breast, sides of neck and eye. HABITAT Subarid thorn scrub near sea level. STATUS Endemic to Madagascar; distributed along a narrow coastal strip in the south-west, where it is common. CALL Vocal during the breeding season, when it utters a descending series of muffled 'boos'.

1 VELVET ASITY   *Philepitta castanea* ■ 16 cm
A chunky dark bird with iridescent, greenish-blue, fleshy caruncles. In non-br.
plumage the overall black colouring is marked with small yellow scales. Female
differs from male in its olive-green plumage marked with pale-yellow blotches on
the underparts, and head marked with a yellow 'moustache' and absence of
caruncles. Juv. similar to ad. female. HABITAT Lower and mid stratum of rain forest
and adjacent secondary forest. Regular member of mixed-species flocks. STATUS
Endemic to Madagascar; found in east and north-east (common), and north-west
(uncommon). CALL A high-pitched, melodious 'psseeeet' whistle.

2 SCHLEGEL'S ASITY   *Philepitta schlegeli* ■ 13 cm
The very large, light-green and blue, fleshy caruncles are highly conspicuous
during breeding season. Distinguished from the male Velvet Asity in its contrasting
black head and yellow underparts. Flight is direct and rapid, the wings producing
a whirring sound. Female differs from male in its yellowish-green plumage
marked with pale-yellow blotches on the underparts, and by the absence of
caruncles. Differs from female Velvet Asity in its pale-green back and yellowish
belly. HABITAT Rain forest, adjacent secondary forest and deciduous dry forest.
STATUS Endemic to Madagascar; common in the north-west; uncommon and
patchily distributed along the west coast. Distribution possibly overlaps with the
Velvet Asity in the north-west. CALL Melodious, high-pitched, 'tsee-tsee-tsee-tsee'
whistle, first rising then falling in volume.

3 COMMON SUNBIRD-ASITY   *Neodrepanis coruscans* ■ 11 cm
Breeding male differs from br. male Yellow-bellied Sunbird-Asity in its duller
yellow underparts streaked with brown across the breast, the yellow fringes to its
wing coverts, and its longer, less decurved bill. The caruncles over the eye are less
extensive, especially in front of eye. Female and juv. differ from female and juv.
Yellow-bellied Sunbird-Asity in their much duller underparts, with yellowish
flash on flanks and undertail. Distinguished from the Souimanga Sunbird and
the Madagascar Green Sunbird (p. 152) by its rounder silhouette, smaller size,
more curved bill, short tail, electric blue upperparts and large, bright-blue and
green caruncles. HABITAT Rain forest and adjacent secondary forest, from low to
mid altitude. STATUS Endemic to Madagascar; occurs in north, east and south-east
parts; common. CALL A high-pitched, five- to eight-note 'see see see see', similar
to that of Yellow-bellied Sunbird-Asity but louder.

4 YELLOW-BELLIED SUNBIRD-ASITY   *Neodrepanis hypoxantha* ■ 10 cm
Breeding male differs from br. male Common Sunbird-Asity in its much brighter
yellow, unmarked underparts, the lack of yellow fringes to its wing coverts, and
its shorter and more deeply decurved bill. The eye caruncles are much more
extensive, especially in front of the eye, where they meet over the bill. Female
and juv. differ from female and juv. Common Sunbird-Asity in the brighter
yellow of their underparts. Distinguished from the Souimanga and Madagascar
Green sunbirds (p. 152) in its much smaller size, rounder silhouette, more curved
bill, short tail, electric-blue upperparts, yellow underparts, and its very large,
bright green and blue caruncles. Flight is direct and rapid, the wings producing a
whirring sound. HABITAT Mid stratum and canopy of the rain forest, from mid to
high altitude. STATUS Endemic to Madagascar; patchily distributed in the island's
north, east and south-east; uncommon. CALL Utters 'see see' notes similar to but
quieter than those of Common Sunbird-Asity.

♂ non-br.

♀

♂

♀

♂

♀

♂

♀

♂

1 Madagascar Bulbul *Hypsipetes madagascariensis* ■ 24 cm
Large, gregarious, noisy and ubiquitous bird with a slender silhouette; brownish-grey except for black cap, orange bill and dark-red eye. Juv. differs from ad. in its duller plumage and darker eye. HABITAT All types of natural forest; also degraded forests, forest plantations, and gardens. Observed in groups; often associated with mixed-flock species. STATUS Endemic to the region and commonly found throughout Madagascar, Aldabra, and the Comoros (four islands). CALL A plaintive, nasal 'eee ooo', decreasing in intensity; and a nasal, bisyllabic, often repeated 'tireet tireet' from a conspicuous perch.

2 Comoro Bulbul *Hypsipetes parvirostris* ■ 25 cm
A large bulbul which could be confused with Madagascar Bulbul but differs in its larger size, the greenish wash to its upperparts and the distinct yellowish wash to underparts. Juv. a dull version of ad. and has a pale-brown bill. Birds on Mohéli have noticeably thicker bills than those found on Grande Comore. HABITAT Found mainly in forest at higher elevations, but also overlaps with Madagascar Bulbul at lower elevations. STATUS Common on Grande Comore and Mohéli. CALL A nasal 'peeeh'.

3 Réunion Bulbul *Hypsipetes borbonicus* ■ 22–24 cm
Unlikely to be mistaken for the similar-sized Red-whiskered Bulbul, which also occurs on Réunion. The obvious dark cap and orangey bill, legs and feet are common to all the region's *Hypsipetes* bulbuls but Réunion species is generally very much darker than the others, has a long bill, a long tail, a shaggy black cap and, a white eye. Not as bold as other closely related bulbuls; more furtive. HABITAT Natural forests at the higher altitudes. STATUS Endemic to Réunion; uncommon. CALL Loud, far-carrying calls of wheezy and nasal phrases.

4 Seychelles Bulbul *Hypsipetes crassirostris* ■ 22–25 cm
The only bulbul found in the central islands of the Seychelles. A large, chunky species with a big, robust bill. Noisy, especially in the evenings on its way to roost or at a fruiting tree. Juv. is duller version of ad. HABITAT Wooded areas, plantations and, less so, lowland gardens. STATUS Common endemic to central Seychelles. CALL A wheezy 'weeee' or 'weeeezup'; reputed to mimic calls of other birds.

5 Mauritius Bulbul *Hypsipetes olivaceus* ■ 22–23 cm
Similar to but highly unlikely to be seen alongside Red-whiskered Bulbul, which has an obvious white cheek patch and crest. Smaller, more compact than the Réunion Bulbul but shares the latter's pinkish-yellow (sometimes orangey) bill, legs and feet and dark cap. HABITAT Natural forests on steep slopes and in gullies. STATUS Uncommon endemic to Mauritius. CALL Various nasal and wheezy calls.

6 Red-whiskered Bulbul *Pycnonotus jocosus* ■ 20 cm
With its dark upperparts, white underparts, conspicuous white cheek-patch and dark crest, this bulbul is unmistakeable. The adult also has a bright red vent and small red patches behind the eyes, features which juv. lacks. HABITAT Varied; from wooded areas and forest edge to gardens, cultivated lands and hedgerows. Avoids dense forests. STATUS Introduced to Mauritius and Réunion (Mascarenes) and Assumption (Seychelles). CALL A varied repertoire of chatters and whistles.

1 APPERT'S GREENBUL   *Bernieria apperti* ■ 15 cm
Medium-sized, slender, almost wholly terrestrial forest bird. The grey head, white throat, yellow breast and belly and its greenish upperparts are diagnostic. HABITAT Leaf litter of deciduous dry forest and adjacent secondary forest, at low elevation. Sometimes associated with mixed-flock species. STATUS Endemic to Madagascar; recently discovered and very localized. Found only in the Zombitse forest (common), and in the Vohibasia forest (uncommon). CALL A thin, high-pitched, often repeated 'tsee tsee', especially when feeding in groups.

2 GREY-CROWNED GREENBUL   *Bernieria cinereiceps* ■ 14 cm
Medium-sized, slender forest passerine characterized by green upperparts, yellow underparts and pale-grey head. Similar to Appert's Greenbul but the two species do not overlap. HABITAT Rain forest. Observed in groups, and often associated with mixed-flock species. Climbs on vertical branches and trunks covered with epiphytic vegetation. STATUS Endemic to Madagascar; occurs in east and locally in north; uncommon. CALL A thin, high-pitched 'tseeet' when feeding.

3 DUSKY GREENBUL   *Bernieria tenebrosa* ■ 14 cm
Medium-sized, secretive understorey forest passerine. The dark-green upperparts, and bright-yellow throat and breast contrasting with the dark-green belly, are diagnostic. Distinguished from Spectacled Greenbul by its smaller size, slimmer silhouette, stockier bill and the strong contrast between yellow throat and dark belly. HABITAT Low stratum of rain forest. Poorly known species; observed individually and sometimes in mixed groups. STATUS Endemic to Madagascar; found in the east, where rare. CALL A soft 'tssit' contact call.

4 LONG-BILLED GREENBUL   *Bernieria madagascariensis* ■ 18–20 cm
Distinguished from Spectacled Greenbul by its larger size, longer bill and duller yellow underparts. Juv. female might be confused with Dusky Greenbul but is larger and has an obvious long, straight bill. HABITAT Rain forest, deciduous dry forest, secondary forest; often associated with mixed-flock species. STATUS Endemic to Madagascar; absent from south but common elsewhere. CALL A harsh, loud 'cheer cheer' when feeding; a more melodious 'chee chee tee tee', decreasing in intensity, from concealed perch.

5 YELLOW-BROWED OXYLABES   *Crossleyia xanthophrys* ■ 15 cm
A medium-sized terrestrial forest passerine with dark-green upperparts, wings and tail, yellow underparts and conspicuously yellow supercilium. Juv. differs from ad. in its duller plumage. HABITAT Leaf litter of rain forest. STATUS Endemic to Madagascar; found in eastern parts, where it is uncommon. CALL A soft, high-pitched 'pit pit'.

6 SPECTACLED GREENBUL   *Bernieria zosterops* ■ 16 cm
This gregarious bird is green above, bright yellow below except for greenish flanks, and has a pale, fleshy lower mandible. Has a conspicuous, incomplete yellow eye-ring. Distinguished from Dusky Greenbul by yellow belly and eye-ring. Juv. differs from ad. in its duller plumage and greenish breast and belly, and could be confused with Dusky Greenbul but is never as dark on the underparts. HABITAT Rain forest and adjacent secondary forest. STATUS Endemic to Madagascar, found in the east, where common. CALL A high-pitched, nasal, unintrusive 'tsee seeseeseesee' when feeding in groups.

1

2

3

juv.

ad. ♀   ad. ♂

4

5

6

131

1 WHITE-THROATED OXYLABES   *Oxylabes madagascariensis* ■ 17 cm
Medium-sized, slender forest passerine, easily identified by chocolate-brown
plumage, white throat, and the thin white stripe across the eye. Juv. differs from
ad. in its dull-brown cap, yellowish-tinged throat and greenish-brown upperparts. HABITAT Leaf litter and lower stratum of evergreen rain forest; generally
found in pairs, often with bird parties. STATUS Endemic to Madagascar; commonly
found in east and north. CALL A melodious 'tsee tseeuu' song.

2 CROSSLEY'S BABBLER   *Mystacornis crossleyi* ■ 16 cm
The contrasting grey, white and black head, black band across eye, and heavy
white 'moustache' are all diagnostic features. Female has less contrasting
plumage and brown top to head. HABITAT Leaf litter of rain forest; generally found
in pairs; walks quietly over forest floor. STATUS Endemic to Madagascar; commonly
found in the east of the island. CALL Utters a distinctive high-pitched, often
repeated, 'tweeeeeeeeee' whistle.

3 MADAGASCAR MAGPIE ROBIN   *Copsychus albospecularis* ■ 18 cm
Not likely to be confused with any other small forest bird; has a distinctive pied
plumage. Three subspecies occur, with variable black and white plumage patterns.
Female is a greyish-brown version of male and might be confused with female
Forest Rock-Thrush (p. 134), but shows a trace of white on shoulders. HABITAT All
types of forest and adjacent secondary forest. STATUS Endemic to Madagascar;
common. CALL Male delivers widely variable series of high-pitched, harmonious
notes from a perch.

4 SEYCHELLES MAGPIE ROBIN   *Copsychus sechellarum* ■ 18–20 cm
A large, thrush-like, black and white bird. Its black plumage has a blueish sheen
when seen in sun. Juv. has rust-coloured markings on wings. Spends most of its
time on the ground, hopping along, often stopping to cock its tail and flick its
wings. HABITAT Frequently seen around human habitation; otherwise found in
thicket and woodland. STATUS Endangered endemic to Frégate and Cousin islands,
and translocated on Aride, in the Seychelles group. CALL Very varied; some hoarse
calls, and a jumbled and melodic song.

5 COMORO THRUSH   *Turdus bewsheri* ■ 22–24 cm
A large thrush (the only one to occur within the region) with olive-brown back
and pale, mottled underparts. In its habitat, cannot be confused with any other
bird. Juv. has mottled plumage. Forages on forest floor or at forest edge, and will
visit fruiting trees. HABITAT Mainly natural forest and forest edge at the higher
elevations. STATUS Common endemic to Grande Comore, Mohéli and Anjouan
islands. CALL A soft contact trill; a melodic, typically thrush-like song.

6 MADAGASCAR HOOPOE   *Upupa marginata* ■ 32 cm
Unmistakeable. In flight it displays large, rounded wings. Female differs from
male in its slightly smaller size and in the beige tinge of parts of the white
plumage. HABITAT Deciduous dry forest; subarid thorn scrub; lightly wooded open
areas; plantations and farmland. STATUS Endemic to Madagascar; found throughout island; common except for east, where rare. CALL A soft but fairly resonant
'rrroooooooooooo' repeated at short intervals from a perch. Individuals respond
to each other's calls.

1 AMBER MOUNTAIN ROCK-THRUSH *Monticola erythronotus* ■ 16 cm
Slender, secretive forest species with greyish-blue head, throat, and nape and orange-rufous (not greyish-blue) mantle, breast, belly, rump and tail. HABITAT Rain forest and adjacent secondary forest. STATUS Endemic to Madagascar; restricted to Amber Mountain in northern region, where common. CALL Melodious; male utters series of high-pitched, harmonious notes.

2 FOREST ROCK-THRUSH *Monticola sharpei* ■ 16 cm
Differs from Amber Mountain Rock-Thrush by greyish-blue (not rufous) mantle and upperbreast. Female brown above except for rufous-brown rump and tail and light brown with brown spots below. Female similar to female Amber Mountain Rock-Thrush. HABITAT Rain forest and adjacent secondary forest, rocky settings with some bushy vegetation. STATUS Endemic to Madagascar; found in east (common), and locally in south-west. CALL Melodious; male utters series of high-pitched, harmonious notes. Species now includes Benson's Rock-Thrush, formerly considered a full species. Recent genetic evidence has shown that birds from rocky outcrops not different from rain-forest individuals.

3 LITTORAL ROCK-THRUSH *Monticola imerinus* ■ 16 cm
Distinguished from the Forest Rock-Thrush by lighter grey upperparts, paler orange underparts, and grey extending to lower breast. Female differs from male in its greyish underparts and pale-grey upperparts marked with dark spots. HABITAT Subarid thorn scrub on sandy coastal soils. STATUS Endemic to Madagascar; found on narrow coastal strip in south, where common. CALL Melodious; male utters series of high-pitched, harmonious notes from conspicuous perch.

4 RÉUNION STONECHAT *Saxicola tectes* ■ 13 cm
A small, conspicuous black and white bird found only at higher elevations on Réunion. Female and juv. are more uniformly brown in colour than ad. male, which varies from brown to almost black. It sits on an exposed perch with a very upright posture and nervous flicking of wings. HABITAT Forest fringes; along paths; on heathlands at the highest elevations. STATUS Common endemic to Réunion Island. CALL A regular contact 'chik chik', and a clipped, musical song.

5 COMMON STONECHAT *Saxicola torquata* ■ 14 cm
A small, plump bird whose underparts are marked by a large, reddish breast-patch. In flight shows a white wingbar, and white uppertail coverts that contrast with dark colour of rest of upperparts. Female differs from male bird in its less contrasting plumage, brown head, whitish underparts and uppertail coverts tinged with orange. HABITAT Open sites with scattered bushes and trees; heathland, wetlands, farmland. STATUS Found on Madagascar and Grande Comore; common. CALL A typical stonechat-like 'chick chick' and jumbled song.

6 NORTHERN (EUROPEAN) WHEATEAR *Oenanthe oenanthe* ■ 15 cm
The breeding male has blue-grey upperparts with black mask. Non-br. male, female and juv. are overall greyish-brown in colour with white rump and diagnostic tail pattern of black tip and central line which forms a distinctive black 'T'. The bird has a very upright stance, hopping over the ground with an occasional 'bob' and wing-flick. HABITAT Prefers lightly wooded open areas, grasslands and sandy stretches. STATUS Rare summer vagrant to Madagascar and the Seychelles. CALL A harsh 'chak chak'.

br. ♂

non-br. ♂

1 WHITE WAGTAIL   *Motacilla alba* ■ 17–18 cm
An unmistakeable small grey and white bird with an especially long tail, which it continuously pumps up and down in a wagging motion. Both br. and non-br. ad. differ from Yellow Wagtail in the absence of any green or yellow in their plumage. Ad. in br. and non-br. plumage shows black cap and breast while juv. is greyish on head and breast. HABITAT Usually associated with wetlands in open areas, but can be found away from water. STATUS Rare summer vagrant to the Seychelles and Réunion. CALL A sparrow-like 'chissik' and softer twitterings.

2 MADAGASCAR WAGTAIL   *Motacilla flaviventris* ■ 19 cm
An elegant, largely terrestrial bird with a slender silhouette. The conspicuously contrasting plumage is grey above, the belly yellow, the white breast crossed by a black band, the long dark tail edged with white. Often found in pairs. Sexes differ slightly; female is paler than male. Juv. differs from ad. in the less conspicuous white supercilium and faint breast-band. HABITAT Typically found near water (rivers, lakes, seashores) and in open areas (rice paddies, gardens); from sea level to very high altitude. STATUS Endemic to Madagascar and found throughout the island, where it is common. CALL Very vocal, giving a characteristic 'tree oo', repeated several times and delivered from ground or in flight.

3 YELLOW WAGTAIL   *Motacilla flava* ■ 16 cm
Can be confused with White Wagtail, which also occurs as a summer vagrant to the region, but differs in the yellowish wash on flanks and belly, and in the absence of greyish or black markings on head and throat. Male head coloration variable according to subspecies. Fairly easily distinguished from Madagascar Wagtail, which is much larger, has a longer tail and a black breast-band. HABITAT Open grassy areas, often near water. STATUS Summer vagrant to the Seychelles. CALL Utters a soft, weak 'tseeep'.

4 TREE PIPIT   *Anthus trivialis* ■ 14–16 cm
Within the region, can be confused only with Red-throated Pipit, and can best be identified by its call. Its plumage is very similar to that of non-br. Red-throated Pipit, but it is less boldly streaked on underparts and has an unmarked (not streaked) rump. When put to flight it will readily alight on a nearby tree or exposed perch. HABITAT Short-grassed areas among stands of trees or shrubs. STATUS Near-annual visitor to the Seychelles group during summer. CALL Sometimes utters a diagnostic 'bzzt' or 'buzzt'.

5 RED-THROATED PIPIT   *Anthus cervinus* ■ 14–15 cm
In its breeding plumage this bird, with its pinkish throat, face and upper breast, is unmistakeable. Non-br. very difficult to tell apart from Tree Pipit, but is noticeably more streaked on underparts, with streaking extending onto belly and flanks. It also has a streaked (not uniform) rump. Unlike Tree Pipit, does not settle in trees. HABITAT Grassy areas, ploughed fields, stony areas. STATUS Summer vagrant to the Seychelles. CALL Utters a thin, high-pitched 'teeez' in flight.

1 non-br.

2 ad.

3 br. ♂

3 non-br. ♂

3 br. ♂

3 br. ♂

5 ♂

4

ad. non-br.

1 HUMBLOT'S FLYCATCHER
Humblotia flavirostris ■ 14 cm

A small flycatcher with a dark cap, pale underparts heavily streaked with dark brown, and a diagnostic yellowish-orange bill. The female is similar to the male but its dark cap is streaked and its breast less so. A silent, unobtrusive bird, usually encountered in pairs. In typical flycatcher fashion it flies out to retrieve its prey, returning to the same perch or one nearby. HABITAT The thicker stands and gullies of natural forest areas. STATUS Uncommon endemic to the higher slopes of Mt. Karthala on Grande Comore. CALL A soft, sharp trill.

2 MADAGASCAR PARADISE FLYCATCHER
Terpsiphone mutata
■ 18–30 cm (plus 12 cm central tail feathers in male)

Elegant, crested, black-hooded forest flycatcher with contrasting coloration. Male has two plumage phases: black and white, and black and rufous. Intermediate (white, and rufous) phases are common. Female is always rufous and black; differs from male in duller coloration, absence of white wingbar, and short tail. HABITAT All types of forest, secondary forest, gardens and tree plantations. STATUS Endemic to the region; commonly found on Madagascar and the Comoros. CALL A harsh 'treeteet treet retreet' followed by a melodious whistle.

3 SPOTTED FLYCATCHER
Musicapa striata ■ 14 cm

Could be confused only with Humblot's Flycatcher, but habitat and range do not overlap. The somewhat similar female Souimanga Sunbird (p. 152) is streaked on the underparts but is much smaller and has a decurved bill. The Spotted Flycatcher has a typical upright posture. Regularly flicks its folded wings. HABITAT Lightly wooded areas, gardens and adjoining paths and roads. STATUS Rare summer vagrant to the Seychelles. CALL A soft 'tzee' and 'zeek chik chik'.

4 SEYCHELLES BLACK PARADISE FLYCATCHER
Terpsiphone corvina
■ 20 cm (plus 16 cm central tail feathers in male)

An unmistakeable species. Male has blue bill and facial skin, long central tail feathers and all-black plumage which, at close range, shows a deep-blue sheen. Female and juv. lack the long tail feathers and have a black head, creamy white underparts and chestnut upperparts and tail. A restless bird, rarely still. HABITAT Lowland woodlands and gardens. STATUS Endangered endemic to La Digue Island, Seychelles group. CALL A harsh 'zweet' alarm and a whistled song.

5 MASCARENE PARADISE FLYCATCHER
Terpsiphone bourbonnensis ■ 15–20 cm

Male has a black cap, rich chestnut back and grey underparts, and lacks the long central tail feathers common to most paradise flycatchers. Bill base and wattle encircling the eye are a deep lilac colour. Black cap absent in female and juv. Male Réunion form has much duller plumage than male Mauritius birds. HABITAT Natural forests, forest edge and secondary growth. STATUS Endemic to Mauritius and Réunion; less common on Mauritius. CALL Typical harsh 'zweet' alarm call and descending whistled trill.

6 WARD'S FLYCATCHER
Pseudobias wardi ■ 15 cm

Can be confused only with Chabert's Vanga (p. 156), but is slimmer and has a black breast-band and large white wingbar. Ambushes prey on the wing. HABITAT Rain forest and adjacent secondary forest. STATUS Endemic to Madagascar; commonly found in the east. CALL A high-pitched, nasal 'tree tree tree' uttered from an unconcealed perch.

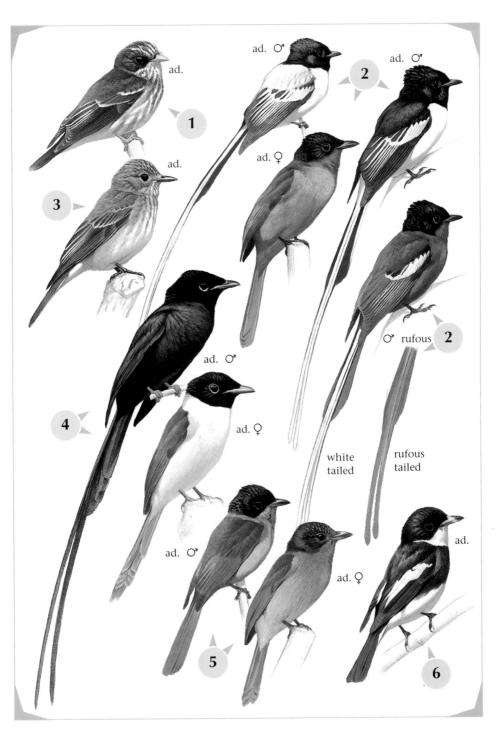

ad.

ad. ♂

2

ad. ♂

3

ad.

ad. ♀

2

♂ rufous

ad. ♂

ad. ♀

white
tailed

rufous
tailed

4

ad. ♂

ad. ♀

5

ad. ♀

ad.

6

139

1 COMMON NEWTONIA　　　　　　　　*Newtonia brunneicauda* ■ 12 cm
A small, plump forest bird with grey upperparts, white underparts tinged with tan, thin black bill, and a pale-yellow (not golden) eye. Distinguished from Dark Newtonia by its greyer upperparts, shorter bill and legs, and pale-yellow eye. HABITAT All original forest types and secondary forest. Found in pairs; frequently associated with bird parties. STATUS Endemic to Madagascar; common. CALL A powerful and often repeated 'kiapakiapakiap'.

2 DARK NEWTONIA　　　　　　　　　*Newtonia amphichroa* ■ 12 cm
A small forest bird with greyish-brown upperparts, white underparts tinged with tan, black bill and golden-yellow eye (though some birds have an all-dark eye). Distinguished from Common Newtonia by its browner upperparts, longer bill and legs, and darker yellow eye. HABITAT Low stratum of rain forest and adjacent secondary growth. STATUS Endemic to Madagascar; found in the east; uncommon except at high altitude. CALL Utters a powerful 'tweedetew tweedetew', repeated many times from a concealed perch; its song is more melodious than that of Common Newtonia.

3 ARCHBOLD'S NEWTONIA　　　　　　　*Newtonia archboldi* ■ 12 cm
Distinguished from Common Newtonia by its darker brown head and upper-parts, and its grey and rufous forehead. HABITAT Subarid thorn scrub; also found very locally in deciduous dry forest near sea level. Observed in pairs. STATUS Endemic to Madagascar; distributed in southern part of island (common), and in parts of south-west (uncommon). CALL A powerful, often repeated 'tekeetee toodee tee' from concealed perch.

4 RED-TAILED NEWTONIA　　　　　　　*Newtonia fanovanae* ■ 12 cm
Differs from Common Newtonia in its rufous tail, and from female Red-tailed Vanga (p. 158) in its smaller size, much thinner bill and absence of pale eye-ring. HABITAT Rain forest. Found in pairs; frequently associated with bird parties. STATUS Endemic to Madagascar; found in east (four sites); from sea level to mid altitude; rare. CALL A high-pitched 'ti-tia-ti-tia-ti-tia', repeated several times.

5 MADAGASCAR CISTICOLA　　　　　　*Cisticola cherina* ■ 12 cm
Small, long-legged warbler with fawn-brown plumage marked by dark stripes above; white below with a graduated white-tipped tail. The region's only cisticola. Juv. differs from ad. in its darker striped upperparts and brown-tinged underparts. HABITAT Bushy vegetation, savannah, surroundings of lakes, highly degraded forest, rice paddies. STATUS Endemic to the region; commonly found on Madagascar, Cosmolédo and Astove. CALL A brief, metallic 'tint tint tint' emitted in flight.

6 MADAGASCAR LARK　　　　　　　　*Mirafra hova* ■ 13 cm
Mainly terrestrial, greyish-brown passerine with light-brown head marked by a large pale supercilium, light-brown upperparts streaked with brown, white underparts streaked with brown on the breast, brown tail with fawn outer tail-feathers, a short, strong, pale bill and long legs. The region's only lark. Typical hovering flight. HABITAT Bushy vegetation, savannah, dry surroundings of lakes, rivers and rice paddies. STATUS Endemic to and common on Madagascar. CALL A series of fluid, melodious notes delivered in flight, more rarely from a perch.

1 MADAGASCAR SWAMP WARBLER   *Acrocephalus newtoni* ■ 18 cm
Large, slender warbler with long straight bill, brown above, whitish below except for throat and chest streaked with brown and rather long, graduated tail. The only reed warbler found in Madagascar. HABITAT Wetland vegetation. STATUS Endemic to Madagascar; common. CALL A series of low-pitched, throaty, melodious notes uttered from a concealed perch, occasionally from a visible reed-top.

2 MADAGASCAR BRUSH WARBLER   *Nesillas typica* ■ 17 cm
Slender, furtive warbler with a straight bill, greyish-brown above, greyish-white below except for a faint lighter supercilium and long, graduated tail. Differs from Subdesert Brush Warbler in its darker upperparts, and from Thamnornis Warbler in its larger size and long, greyish-brown graduated tail. Individuals from Anjouan (Comoros) are more olivaceous on the upperparts. HABITAT All original forest types and secondary growth except subarid thorn scrub, where replaced by Subdesert Brush Warbler. STATUS Endemic to the region; absent in south of island, common elsewhere. Also commonly found on Mohéli and Anjouan. CALL A succession of rapid-fire 'treek treek treek' notes.

3 THAMNORNIS WARBLER   *Thamnornis chloropetoides* ■ 15 cm
Slender warbler with straight bill, pale greyish-green above, whitish below, head marked by a lighter supercilium, and graduated, white-tipped tail. HABITAT Subarid thorn scrub; locally in deciduous dry forest, adjacent secondary growth. Associated with mixed flocks in the understorey vegetation and leaf litter. STATUS Endemic to Madagascar; commonly found in south and south-west. CALL A 'dew dew dew dew' whistle preceded by a buzzing 'geeer' note.

4 SUBDESERT BRUSH WARBLER   *Nesillas lantzii* ■ 17 cm
Slender, furtive warbler with straight bill, pale brownish-grey above, greyish-white below except for a lighter supercilium and long graduated tail. Very similar to the Madagascar Brush Warbler; differs in its lighter pale-grey upperparts. Distinguished from Thamnornis Warbler by its larger size and long, greyish-brown, graduated tail. HABITAT Subarid thorn scrub, gallery forest, secondary growth, gardens. STATUS Endemic to Madagascar; found in the south, where common. CALL A succession of more rapid, higher-pitched 'trreeeek trreeeek trreeeek' notes than Madagascar Brush Warbler.

5 GREY EMUTAIL   *Amphilais seebohmi* ■ 17 cm
Slender, secretive warbler with brownish-grey plumage marked with dark-brown streaks, and a long, graduated tail which appears shaggy and worn. Flies in short stretches; difficult to observe as it moves quickly in tangled vegetation. HABITAT Dense marshland vegetation adjacent to rain forest from low to very high altitude. STATUS Endemic to Madagascar; found in the east, where uncommon. CALL A melodious, loud 'teoo teoo teoo' whistle preceded by a harsh 'cherr'.

6 BROWN EMUTAIL   *Dromaeocercus brunneus* ■ 15 cm
Slender, secretive warbler with chocolate-brown plumage, white throat, and a long, graduated, shaggy tail. Flies in short stretches just above ground level; difficult to observe as it moves quickly in the tangled ground vegetation. HABITAT Dense understorey of rain forest; from sea level to high altitude. STATUS Endemic to Madagascar; found in the east; uncommon. CALL A loud, high-pitched 'tuik tuik tuik tia tia' whistle, usually uttered from a concealed perch.

1 RODRIGUES WARBLER   *Acrocephalus rodericanus* ■ 13,5 cm
The only warbler on Rodrigues and unlikely to be confused with any other species. Uniformly olive-brown on back with paler, yellowish-buff underparts. Bill long and flesh-coloured at base. Feathers on head erectile, giving the bird a crested appearance. Tail habitually jerked up and down. Does not hide in undergrowth but is bold, inquisitive (to pishing noises) and unafraid to venture into the open. HABITAT Remnant patches of woodland on slopes and in gullies. STATUS Endemic to Rodrigues, Mascarenes group, where it survives in small numbers. CALL Harsh chattering alarm call and loud, melodious song.

2 SEYCHELLES WARBLER   *Acrocephalus sechellensis* ■ 14 cm
A dull olive-brown warbler with pale buffy-yellow underparts and obscure buff eyebrow stripe. Bill is long and horn-coloured with yellowish fleshy base; legs are a blue-grey colour. Noisy and bold; does not skulk in cover, either flits about in unconcerned fashion in undergrowth or ventures out into the open. Flicks tail up and down when moving through thickets. HABITAT Scrubby undergrowth in light woodlands and thickets. STATUS Endemic to Seychelles, where it is found on Cousin, Cousine and Aride islands. CALL Melodious song; alarm call a brisk chatter.

3 ALDABRA BRUSH WARBLER   *Nesillas aldabrana* ■ 18–20 cm
The only warbler of its size likely to be encountered on Aldabra. A peculiarly cigar-shaped bird with very short wings, uniformly dun in colour with paler underparts and a noticeably long, pointed tail. Very shy and retiring, and most likely to be located by its call. HABITAT Dense, often impenetrable thicket. STATUS Endemic to Aldabra, found only on Middle Island, last seen in 1967 and probably extinct. CALL Song has never been described but probably harsh as in other Nesillas warblers. Call is a nasal, three-syllable chirrup.

4 COMORO BRUSH WARBLER   *Nesillas brevicaudata* ■ 18–20 cm
Very similar to other brush warblers on the Comoro Islands but the only one found on Grande Comore, so there should be no confusion. It is a uniform dull olive-brown colour above with paler underparts, and has a long tail, which it jerks up and down in unusual fashion, and a long, pale-based bill. This species is very much bolder than the Madagascar Brush Warbler (p. 142), moving around in trees and thickets at the higher altitudes. It can also be seen in the canopy. HABITAT Natural forests on the slopes of Mt. Karthala and on the edges of high-elevation heathlands. STATUS Not uncommon on the higher ground on Mt. Karthala, Grande Comore. CALL A harsh 'chik chik' and a jumbled series of chatters and musical phrases.

5 BENSON'S BRUSH WARBLER   *Nesillas mariae* ■ 18–20 cm
Can be confused with the Madagascar Brush Warbler (p. 142), which also occurs on Mohéli Island, Comoros. Differs in its more olive-green (not brown) upperparts and its plain (unmarked) face. Behaviour very different, more bold, hopping about 2–6-m-high tree branches in the open in contrast to the Madagascar Brush Warbler, which skulks in the undergrowth and is difficult to see. HABITAT Natural forested slopes and gullies. STATUS Common endemic to Mohéli Island, Comoros. CALL Contact call is a loud 'priip' and a fast 'ti ti ti ti'. Song a jumbled warbling of chips and musical phrases.

1 COMMON JERY   *Neomixis tenella* ■ 10 cm
Small, plump, forest bird with a short, straight, thin bill and a light-brown eye, yellowish-green above, whitish below except for yellowish breast marked with faint, darker streaks, and a grey nape. Juv. differs from ad. in its duller plumage and darker eye. HABITAT All natural forest types and secondary forest. Observed in groups; often associated with mixed-flock species. STATUS Endemic to Madagascar; very common. CALL A high-pitched 'tsee seeseeseesee'.

2 STRIPE-THROATED JERY   *Neomixis striatigula* ■ 12 cm
Distinguished from Common Jery, Green Jery, and Cryptic Warbler by its larger size, longer dark bill, partly streaked underparts and diffused yellow supercilium. HABITAT All original types of forest and adjacent secondary forest. Seen individually and in mixed-species flocks. STATUS Endemic to Madagascar; common. CALL A rising and falling 'tche tche tche tche tche tche' uttered in early morning.

3 GREEN JERY   *Neomixis viridis* ■ 10,5 cm
Small, plump, furtive forest bird. Distinguished from Common Jery by its green nape and whitish underparts; from Stripe-throated Jery by its smaller size and plain yellow throat, and from Cryptic Warbler by its light-coloured legs. Juv. differs from ad. in its darker eye. HABITAT Rain forest. Often associated with mixed-species flocks. STATUS Endemic to Madagascar; found in the east; uncommon. CALL A monotonous, often repeated 'tchee chee che che che che' whistle.

4 WEDGE-TAILED JERY   *Hartertula flavoviridis* ■ 12 cm
A small, fairly gregarious forest bird, olive-green above, bright yellow below except for green undertail coverts. Distinguished from all jery species by its larger size, grey cheek, plain bright-yellow underparts and graduated tail, and from Spectacled Greenbul (p. 130) by its smaller size, brighter yellow underparts and graduated tail. HABITAT Rain forest. Observed in small groups; also associated with mixed-species flocks. STATUS Endemic to Madagascar; found in the east, where uncommon. CALL A shrill, nasal 'tsee zeezeezeezee' uttered when moving.

5 RAND'S WARBLER   *Randia pseudozosterops* ■ 12 cm
Distinguished from Stripe-throated Jery by plain pale underparts and conspicuous pale supercilium. HABITAT Rain forest and adjacent secondary forest. Frequently associated with mixed-species flocks, and especially with Stripe-throated Jery. STATUS Endemic to Madagascar; found in east, where common. CALL A series of energetic, rising and falling 'sooo sooo seee seee' notes, uttered in early morning from a perch, often a dead twig emerging from the canopy, sometimes in company of Stripe-throated Jery.

6 CRYPTIC WARBLER   *Cryptosylvicola randrianasoloi* ■ 11,5 cm
Small forest bird with olive-green upperparts and greyish-yellow underparts, thin black and orange bill, and pale legs. Distinguished from Common and Green jeries by larger size, unmarked plumage coloration, pale legs and partly orange lower mandible, and from Stripe-throated Jery by smaller size, plain underparts and dark legs. HABITAT Rain forest and adjacent secondary forest. STATUS Endemic to Madagascar, recently discovered (1995), distributed in east, where common. CALL A series of raspy, high-pitched, slightly slurred, monotone 'tsetsetsetse' sounds, repeated from perch; dominant call in canopy.

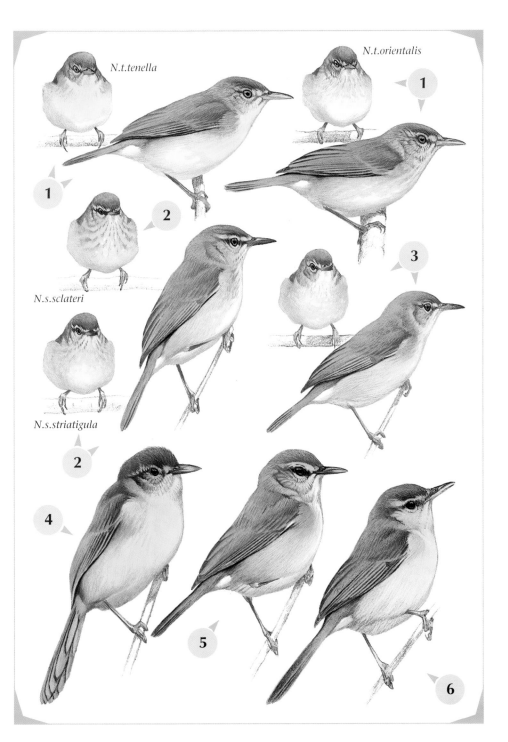

N.t.tenella

N.t.orientalis

N.s.sclateri

N.s.striatigula

1 KIRK'S WHITE-EYE
Zosterops kirki ■ 11 cm

Can be mistaken only for Karthala White-eye, which is also found on Grande Comore. Their respective ranges, however, are mutually exclusive: Kirk's White-eye is confined to woodland, and is not present on the heathlands of Mt. Karthala. Very much more yellow on the face and underparts and greener on the back than Karthala White-eye. HABITAT Forests and secondary growth, but avoids heathland at higher elevations. STATUS Common endemic to Grande Comore. CALL Typical white-eye whistled notes and song.

2 KARTHALA WHITE-EYE
Zosterops mouroniensis ■ 13 cm

Gregarious small passerine with olive-green upperparts, wings and tail, yellow throat and undertail coverts and white eye-ring. The only white-eye to occur on the heathlands of Mt. Karthala. Kirk's White-eye, which is brighter yellow in colour, might be seen on forest edge at high elevations but does not penetrate the forest. Juv. differs from ad. in its duller plumage and smaller eye-ring. HABITAT Short colonizing woodland and heathland on the higher laval scree slopes. STATUS Common endemic at high elevations and to the summit of Mt. Karthala, Grande Comore. CALL A typical, mellow, white-eye 'fee fee fee pee pee' contact whistle.

3 MAYOTTE WHITE-EYE
Zosterops mayottensis ■ 11 cm

The only white-eye found on Mayotte Island, Comoros. It displays typical white-eye behaviour, occurring in small groups, continually keeping vocal contact as the birds follow each other through trees and shrubs. More often seen in the drier eastern side of Mayotte; less common in patches of rain forest. HABITAT Frequents both forest and more open woodland. STATUS Common endemic of Mayotte. CALL Typical white-eye sounds.

4 MADAGASCAR WHITE-EYE
Zosterops maderaspatanus ■ 12 cm

Small, gregarious passerine with yellowish-green upperparts, wings and tail; bright-yellow throat and undertail coverts, and a conspicuous white eye-ring. Distinguished from Common, Green, and Stripe-throated jeries and Cryptic Warbler (p. 146) by its larger size, plain bright-yellow throat and undertail coverts, and white eye ring. Juv. differs from ad. in its duller plumage and smaller eye-ring. HABITAT Low, mid and upper strata of all original forest types, including mangrove and high-altitude scrub; secondary forest, parks and gardens; from sea level to very high altitude. A forest species well adapted to man-made woody environment. Observed in groups; frequently associated with mixed flocks in which the Madagascar White-eye is often the dominant species. STATUS Endemic to the region and commonly found on Madagascar, the Seychelles (Aldabra, Cosmolédo and Astove) and the Comoros, Anjouan and Mohéli. CALL Vocal; utters melodious song from unconcealed perch; and a faint 'wee tseet'.

1 MAURITIUS OLIVE WHITE-EYE   *Zosterops chloronothus* ■ 10 cm
Differs from the very common Mauritius Grey White-eye in the obvious white ring encircling the eye and its noticeably decurved bill. It is also overall olive-green (not grey) in colour and lacks the grey rump and white vent of the Mauritius Grey White-eye. HABITAT Natural forest and scrub; avoids gardens and invasive stands of woodland. STATUS Uncommon endemic to the south-west parts of Mauritius. CALL A metallic 'plik plik' contact note and warbled song.

2 RÉUNION OLIVE WHITE-EYE   *Zosterops olivaceus* ■ 11 cm
Differs from Réunion Grey White-eye in its much darker appearance, the obvious white ring around the eye, its decurved bill and its dark (not pale) rump. Close observation shows that the blackish forehead and white eye-ring do not meet in front of the eye. HABITAT Natural forest at higher altitudes. STATUS Common endemic on Réunion Island, Mascarenes. CALL Contact call a clipped 'chip chip'; flight call a 'chuck chuck'.

3 SEYCHELLES WHITE-EYE   *Zosterops modestus* ■ 10 cm
This tiny bird is the only white-eye found on the Seychelles islands of Mahé and Conception. It is a dull olive-grey species with paler underparts, a tiny, sharp bill and inconspicuous white eye-ring. Occurs in small groups and, in typical white-eye behaviour, flits about nervously in trees and shrubs while giving its contact calls. HABITAT Prefers secondary habitat with alien trees and shrubs. STATUS Endangered endemic to Mahé, in the Seychelles group. Recently discovered on Conception, a small island offshore of Mahé, where it is common. CALL A soft, trilling note and clipped 'tik tik' contact calls.

4 MAURITIUS GREY WHITE-EYE   *Zosterops mauritianus* ■ 10 cm
The most common and conspicuous of Mauritius's white-eyes. Differs from Mauritius Olive White-eye in its overall much greyer, less olive appearance, its pale (not dark) rump and its less noticeable white eye-ring. It also has a short, straight (not sharp, decurved) bill. HABITAT Natural forests to secondary growth, stands of alien vegetation and gardens. STATUS Common endemic to Mauritius. CALL Contact notes a plaintive 'plee plee plee'; song a whistled warbling.

5 RÉUNION GREY WHITE-EYE   *Zosterops borbonicus* ■ 10 cm
Differs from Réunion Olive White-eye in its overall paler and much greyer (not olive-green) plumage, its white (not dark) rump, brighter orange flanks and the brownish wash to its mantle. The species is in fact very variable in overall colour but is never as dark as Réunion Olive White-eye and always has a pale rump. An unusual feature of both these white-eyes is the 'epaulette' effect created by the obvious pale stripe running down the sides of puffed-out breast and flanks. This feature is much more noticeable on Réunion Grey White-eye. HABITAT Natural forests at higher altitudes, seasonally at lower elevations in exotic vegetation. STATUS Common endemic to Réunion Island, Mascarenes. CALL Varied 'chee chee chee' contact notes; song a varied warble.

1 MADAGASCAR GREEN SUNBIRD   *Nectarinia notata* ■ 14 cm

A large sunbird with metallic blue-green head, throat, upperbreast, and mantle, and blackish wings, belly, and tail. Distinguished from the Souimanga Sunbird by its much larger size, longer bill and overall dark underparts. Non-br. male is similar to female except for a few scattered metallic-blue feathers. Female differs from male in its grey-brown head with lighter supercilium, and underparts that are greyish with brown dots. Differs from female Souimanga Sunbird in its much larger size, longer bill and marked underparts. Juv. distinguished from female by shorter bill and solid-grey chin, throat and chest. HABITAT Mid and upper stratum of all original forest types, including mangrove, secondary forest, parks and gardens; from sea level to high altitude. A forest species well adapted to a man-made woody environment. Observed in pairs. STATUS Endemic to the region; on Madagascar (common); and on Mohéli in the Comoros, where common. CALL A vocal species, uttering a high-pitched, resonant, repeated 'twee twee twee twee' from a visible perch.

2 COMORO GREEN SUNBIRD   *Nectarinia moebii* ■ 14,5–15 cm

Larger than Madagascar Green Sunbird; also differs in its vividly iridescent purplish-blue (not green) throat and breast. Female is a paler buffy-yellow on the underparts, with much less streaking than on underparts of female Madagascar Green Sunbird. HABITAT Forests and secondary growth. STATUS Common endemic to Grande Comore Island. CALL 'Tsee tsee' song is similar to that of Madagascar Green Sunbird but higher pitched.

3 SEYCHELLES SUNBIRD   *Nectarinia dussumieri* ■ 12 cm

The only sunbird occurring in the central Seychelles and unlikely to be confused with any other similar-sized species. When seen in bright sunlight, male has a deep-blue throat and breast and, when alarmed, flashes bright-yellow pectoral tufts. Female is dull brown with paler underparts. In flight, both sexes show conspicuous white tip to tail. HABITAT Has adapted to a wide range of secondary and alien habitats. STATUS Common endemic to central Seychelles. CALL Typical sunbird 'tisk tisk' contact calls and jumbled song.

4 HUMBLOT'S SUNBIRD   *Nectarinia humbloti* ■ 11 cm

The male has olive-green upperparts and metallic greeny-blue throat and breast, with bright-yellow pectoral tufts when excited or alarmed. Female is drab, with yellow underparts and streaked breast. Smaller than Madagascar Green Sunbird and Comoro Green Sunbird, and has a shorter bill. HABITAT Forests and secondary growth. STATUS Common endemic to Grande Comore and Mohéli. CALL Typical scolding 'tssk tsssk' notes and jumbled chippy song.

1 SOUIMANGA SUNBIRD

Nectarinia souimanga ■ 10 cm

A very small bird with a metallic-green head, throat and mantle; a long, curved, thin, black bill; a metallic-blue chest separated from the bright yellow belly by a red breast-band. Distinguished from the Madagascar Green Sunbird by its much smaller size, yellow belly and red breast-band. Non-br. male lacks metallic sheen to head, throat, mantle and chest. Distinguished from Common Sunbird-Asity (p. 126) and the Yellow-bellied Sunbird-Asity (p. 126) by its slender silhouette, larger size, less curved bill, longer tail, and the metallic sheen to its plumage. Female differs from male in its green-grey head marked with a faint supercilium, dull olive-green upperparts, greyish chin dotted with dark grey, and dull-yellow flanks and belly. Juv. differs from female in its duller plumage. HABITAT Low, mid and upper stratum of all original forest types, including mangrove and high-altitude scrub; secondary forest; parks and gardens; from sea level to very high altitude. A forest species well adapted to man-made woody environment. Observed in pairs. STATUS Endemic to the region and common on Madagascar and Aldabra. CALL A very vocal species, uttering a plaintive 'teeeeee' followed by a resonant 'teeteeteetee' repeated at regular intervals.

2 ABBOTT'S SUNBIRD

Nectarinia abbotti ■ 10 cm

Similar in size and shape to Souimanga Sunbird (p. 152) but has a black (not yellow) belly and vent. The wine-coloured breast-band is a deeper red than that of Souimanga Sunbird, and the pectoral tufts are bright yellow. Female is overall darker than female Souimanga Sunbird, has duller yellow underparts and a black throat barred with buff. Birds on Assumption are slightly smaller than those on Astove and Cosmolédo islands. HABITAT Coastal scrub, light woodland and thicket. STATUS Common endemic to the Aldabras, where it is found on Cosmolédo, Astove and Assumption islands. CALL Typical sunbird 'chissik' sounds and a warbling song interspersed with harsher notes.

3 ANJOUAN SUNBIRD

Nectarinia comorensis ■ 10 cm

The male is a very dark sunbird, appearing all-black when seen in shade. In sunlight the back of the head, throat and breast are an iridescent greeny-blue. The belly is black. When alarmed and excited it flashes its bright-orange pectoral tufts. Female a dull olive-green with uniformly paler underparts. HABITAT Virtually any part of Anjouan Island where there are stands of thicket and forest. STATUS Common endemic throughout Anjouan Island, Comoros. CALL A sharp 'pit pit' contact call and variable jumbled song.

4 MAYOTTE SUNBIRD

Nectarinia coquerellii ■ 10 cm

The male has a brightly coloured orange and yellow belly, which contrasts with the iridescent metallic greeny-blue of the breast and upperparts. By far the most attractive sunbird in the region. Female is a uniform olive colour with slightly paler underparts. HABITAT Prefers more open areas and forest edge; avoids dense forest. STATUS Common endemic to Mayotte Island, Comoros. CALL A typical sunbird mix of harsh chipping notes and song.

1 NUTHATCH VANGA
Hypositta corallirostris ■ 13 cm

This small nuthatch-like vanga, with its overall blue-grey colour and bright red bill, is unmistakeable. Female and juv. are duller versions of male, showing a brownish-washed face and throat and a dull-red bill. Like a nuthatch, the bird climbs up and along tree-trunks and branches with a jerky motion, its progress always upwards and forwards, but does not climb down the trunks. Flies in undulating fashion between trees. Almost always found in pairs or small groups within bird parties, foraging from mid stratum to canopy, very rarely at the lower levels. HABITAT Rain forests and adjacent secondary growth, from sea level to high altitude. STATUS Endemic to Madagascar; confined to the east, where locally common. CALL A faint 'tseep tseep' contact call.

2 WHITE-HEADED VANGA
Leptopterus viridis ■ 20 cm

Black and white in colour. In flight could be mistaken at a distance for Sickle-billed Vanga (p. 158) but is very much smaller, and flies more rapidly and directly with an action quite unlike that of the bigger bird (which has broad, rounded wings that it uses laboriously). Female has a greyish (not white) head; juv. has dark back barred with pale brown. Frequently encountered in bird parties and occurs alongside large gatherings of Sickle-billed Vangas. HABITAT All natural forest types and adjacent secondary growth. STATUS Endemic to Madagascar; commonly found throughout the island. CALL Very noisy; characteristic 'yippee hoo' whistle and variations thereon.

3 CHABERT'S VANGA
Leptopterus chabert ■ 14 cm

This small black and white bird is unlikely to be confused with any other species except perhaps Madagascar Blue Vanga, and then only at a distance. The pale-blue bill and bright-blue eye-ring are very noticeable at close range. Juv. has upperparts mottled with white. Occurs in small groups and has a 'follow my leader' flight movement. HABITAT All natural wooded and forested areas, secondary growth and exotic plantations. STATUS Endemic to Madagascar; the most common vanga; found throughout the island. CALL Utters a 'tse tse push' flight call with variations.

4 MADAGASCAR BLUE VANGA
Cyanolanius madagascarinus ■ 16 cm

A dazzling blue and white vanga, and quite unmistakeable. Can be confused with Chabert's Vanga at long range, but latter is jet-black and white (not blue and white). When seen close to, pale-blue bill and eye and the black chin-patch are noticeable. Juv. is a duller version of ad., with a dark bill and eye. A prominent and highly visual member of bird parties, most often occurring in pairs or small family groups. HABITAT Natural forest, secondary growth and adjacent scrub. STATUS Endemic to Madagascar; common except in the south, where absent. CALL A harsh 'teea teea teea', repeated often.

5 COMORO BLUE VANGA
Cyanolanius comorensis ■ 17–19 cm

Larger than Madagascar Blue Vanga, with a uniform lilac-blue across the head, back and rump with no contrast between crown and back. Bill is also longer and thinner. Juv. is duller but has uniform blue on upperparts and almost uniform warm buff underparts. HABITAT All types of woodland and coastal scrub. STATUS Common endemic to Mohéli and very rare and possibly extinct on Grande Comore, Comoro Islands. CALL Softer contact notes than Madagascar Blue Vanga, and a more prolonged 'teea teea teea' call.

1 HELMET VANGA *Euryceros prevostii* ■ 29 cm
Unmistakeable vanga with a massive, pale-blue bill. Juv. is dull rufous-brown with black tail and flight feathers and a less well-developed black (not blue) bill. Regularly found in pairs and small family groups. HABITAT Undisturbed rain forest. STATUS Endemic to Madagascar; found in the east and north-east; uncommon. CALL An often repeated 'trewdew trewdew trewdew' call.

2 SICKLE-BILLED VANGA *Falculea palliata* ■ 32 cm
The combination of black and white plumage and long, grey, decurved bill is diagnostic. Juv. is similar to ad. but has light-brown barring on its black back. Flight action is laboured, the large, rounded wings producing a loud whooshing sound. Clings to branches and trunks, using its long bill to probe into crevices and bark. HABITAT Deciduous dry forest, subarid thorn scrub and thicket. STATUS Endemic to Madagascar; common in south, west and north. CALL Continuous 'wa ha wa ha' contact call; a nasal 'gaaa gaaa gaaa' flight call uttered by group.

3 RUFOUS VANGA *Schetba rufa* ■ 20 cm
An unmistakeable shrike-like bird, distinguished by its bright-rufous, black and white plumage. Female differs from male in its black cap, white throat and white breast. Juv. a duller version of female. HABITAT Rain forest and deciduous dry forest. STATUS Endemic to Madagascar; locally common in east, west and north. CALL A repeated 'troodoo troodoo troodoo' and loud bill-clacking.

4 BERNIER'S VANGA *Oriolia bernieri* ■ 23 cm
A little-known and rarely seen vanga, which could be mistaken only for a Crested Drongo (p. 164) but lacks the latter's crest, is entirely different in shape, has a conical, pale bill and lacks the forked tail. Female and juv. are ginger-rufous heavily barred with black. Seen mostly in small flocks, and often joins large bird parties. HABITAT Undisturbed rain forest. STATUS Endemic to Madagascar; confined to the east and north-east, where rare. CALL A loud, Greenshank-like 'cheww', but most often located in flight, when its wing-beats produce a loud, whirring sound.

5 RED-SHOULDERED VANGA *Calicalicus rufocarpalis* ■ 15 cm
Can be confused only with the Red-tailed Vanga, from which the male differs in its larger size, longer tail and bill and, when seen close to, its pale (not dark) eye, which is diagnostic. Female very similar to female Red-tailed Vanga but is larger and has a reddish (not brown) shoulder and a pale (not dark) eye. Juv. not described. HABITAT Very little known; includes subarid thorn scrub near sea level. STATUS Unknown. Described in 1997 from birds observed near Toliara in south-west Madagascar. Endemic. CALL Unknown.

6 RED-TAILED VANGA *Calicalicus madagascariensis* ■ 13–14 cm
An easily identified small vanga with reddish wings and tail and contrasting grey, black and white plumage. Female could be confused with Common and Red-tailed newtonias (p. 140) but differs from both in its larger size, dark (not pale) eye, obvious pale eye-ring and stout, conical bill. Differs from very similar female Red-shouldered Vanga in its smaller size, shorter tail, reddish (not brown) shoulder and dark (not pale) eye. HABITAT Various wet and dry forest types, secondary forest. STATUS Endemic to Madagascar; distributed throughout the island except the southern part; common. CALL A wolf-whistle-like 'weet weeeoo', often repeated

ad.

1

juv.

juv.

2

ad.

3

♀

♂

4

♀

♂

5

♀

♂

6

♀

♂

1 LAFRESNAYE'S VANGA   *Xenopirostris xenopirostris* ■ 24 cm
Within its range, could be confused only with Madagascar Cuckoo Shrike (p. 162), from which it differs in its larger size, massive pale-grey bill and white (not grey) underparts. Range does not overlap with that of similar Van Dam's Vanga. Female shows a black cap but also the large, pale-grey bill, often showing a gap between mandibles. Juv. similar to female but has light-brown barring on mantle. Mostly encountered in pairs and very often in bird parties. HABITAT Subarid thorn scrub and adjacent secondary habitat at sea level to low altitude. STATUS Endemic to Madagascar; confined to southern parts of island, where it is common. CALL Most often located by its diagnostic call, an often-repeated 'tssee oo' whistle which decreases in intensity.

2 HOOK-BILLED VANGA   *Vanga curvirostris* ■ 25–29 cm
Easily identified large, black and white vanga. Diagnostic features include a large, robust and fiercely hooked bill, and a white head with black crown. In flight shows a conspicuous white wingbar and a black tail tipped with grey and white. Juv. has greyish head and underparts, and black back feathers edged with pale brown. HABITAT All types of original forest and secondary forest. STATUS Endemic to Madagascar; common. CALL A diagnostic, long drawn-out, often repeated 'teeeuuu' whistle; flight call a fluted 'teeu teeu teeu'.

3 POLLEN'S VANGA   *Xenopirostris polleni* ■ 24 cm
Can be confused only with the Tylas, from which it differs in its larger size, more robust build and massive, pale-grey, hooked bill. Some birds have almost white underparts, with only a tinge of orange. Female similar to male but with black restricted to throat. Juv. is a dull version of female with a weaker bill. Found in pairs or small family groups; regular member of bird parties. HABITAT Rain forests. STATUS Uncommon endemic to Madagascar; confined to east. CALL Whistled 'tsseee ooo', very similar to calls of Van Dam's and Lafresnaye's vangas.

4 VAN DAM'S VANGA   *Xenopirostris damii* ■ 23 cm
Within its range can be confused only with Tylas but is larger and more robust, with an unmistakeably massive, pale-grey, hooked bill and paler underparts. Although very similar to Lafresnaye's Vanga the two species do not overlap. Female differs from male in its white (not black) forehead. Juv. similar to female but with light-brown barring on the mantle. Frequently encountered in pairs in bird parties, often in company with Rufous Vanga (p. 158). HABITAT Deciduous dry forest at low altitude. STATUS Endemic to Madagascar; known only from two areas; uncommon in the western area, rare in northern one. CALL A sharp, piercing 'tsee oo', similar to whistle of Lafresnaye's Vanga.

5 TYLAS   *Tylas eduardi* ■ 21 cm
Occurs alongside Pollen's Vanga and can be confused with that bird, which it is thought to mimic. Differs in its smaller size and thinner, unhooked bill. Some Tylas individuals are almost entirely white on the underparts, with only a faint tinge of orange. The western race, *T. e. albigularis*, is much paler with an olive-grey back, the female easily distinguished by its black cap and grey throat. HABITAT Rain forests, deciduous dry forests, and adjacent secondary growth. STATUS Endemic to Madagascar; restricted to and common in the eastern rain forests. The western race is highly localized, rare, and considered by some to be a full species. CALL A repetitive 'weeet weeet weeoo'.

western race ♂

eastern race ♂

1 MADAGASCAR CUCKOO SHRIKE   *Coracina cinerea* ■ 24 cm
Robust, medium-sized, short-tailed black and grey bird reminiscent of a vanga. Male has black head and grey body, and darker grey wings and tail. Female differs from male in its grey head and throat and lighter-grey upperparts. Juv. differs from female in its upperparts and upperwing coverts edged with light brown. HABITAT All original forest and adjacent secondary growth; often associated with vangas. STATUS Endemic to and common on Madagascar. CALL A series of liquid, fluted 'cheekee keedee dee dee dee' notes, decreasing in intensity.

2 RÉUNION CUCKOO SHRIKE   *Coracina newtoni* ■ 22 cm
Réunion's only cuckoo shrike. Male is uniformly grey with black mask, wings and white-tipped tail. Female and juv. brownish on the back with narrow white eyebrow stripe, and paler underparts finely barred black. Extremely shy and furtive, usually detected by call. HABITAT Natural forests at high altitudes, and steep, forested gullies. STATUS Uncommon endemic to Réunion, confined to north-west. CALL Male has clear whistled 'tui tui tui'; female a harsh, scolding call.

3 MAURITIUS CUCKOO SHRIKE   *Coracina typica* ■ 22 cm
The male is similar to male Réunion Cuckoo Shrike, but darker. By contrast female is markedly different, with very dark rufous on upperparts and a uniform paler rufous below. Juv., which has finely barred underparts, resembles both female and juv. Réunion Cuckoo Shrike. HABITAT Natural forests and thick natural scrub. STATUS Uncommon endemic to Mauritius; restricted to forest patches in south-west. CALL A musical trilling; alarm note is a harsh 'tschrek'.

4 COMORO CUCKOO SHRIKE   *Coracina cucullata* ■ 24 cm
Both male and female are very similar to but smaller than Madagascar Cuckoo Shrike, and have almost white (not grey) underparts, and different calls and songs. Moreover, unique to this species is an olive morph, which resembles the ordinary cuckoo shrike in shape and behaviour but has olive-green colouring above and on throat and primrose-yellow underparts. HABITAT Natural forests, forest edge and scrub. STATUS Uncommon endemic to Grande Comore and Mohéli. CALL A softer series of 'cheekee keedee' notes than Madagascar Cuckoo Shrike's.

5 MADAGASCAR STARLING   *Hartlaubius auratus* ■ 20cm
Differs from Madagascar Bulbul (p. 128) in its smaller size, showing a conspicuous white wing-patch and, in flight, white outer tail-feathers. Female is duller brown with streaked underparts. HABITAT Rain forest, deciduous dry forest and adjacent secondary forest, subarid thorn scrub and gallery forest. STATUS Endemic to Madagascar; common in east and north, uncommon in west, rare in south. CALL Quiet species; utters harmonious, repeated, four-syllable 'too teeteetee'.

6 COMMON MYNAH   *Acridotheres tristis* ■ 25 cm
The only mynah-type bird in the region; unlikely to be confused with superficially similar Madagascar Starling because of its much larger size and entirely different behaviour. It further differs in its much larger white wing-patches and the very noticeable white tip to the tail. HABITAT Mainly in association with human habitation; often alongside livestock. STATUS Introduced to most of the larger islands within the region. CALL Jumbled titters and chatters.

1 CRESTED DRONGO
Dicrurus forficatus ■ 26 cm

Large, slightly glossy black bird with a long forked tail and erect feathers on forehead. Flight is rapid and acrobatic. Often mobs mammals and other large birds. Juv. differs from ad. in white-mottled underparts and upperwing coverts. HABITAT All original forest types and secondary forest; wooded savanna. Plays an important role in mixed-flock groups. STATUS Endemic to the region, where found on Madagascar, and Anjouan in the Comoros, where common. CALL A wide variety of loud calls and whistles.

2 MAYOTTE DRONGO
Dicrurus waldenii ■ 28 cm

The region's largest drongo, with an unusually deep forked tail, the outer tail feathers slightly splayed out and curved to give an exaggerated long-tail impression. Lacks the crest of Crested Drongo, which is found on neighbouring island of Anjouan. Juv. is duller version of ad. HABITAT Natural forest; degraded scrub and plantations. STATUS A locally common endemic to Mayotte Island, Comoros. CALL A soft 'plitt plitt' when hawking insects; song jumbled and coarse.

3 ALDABRA DRONGO
Dicrurus aldabranus ■ 24 cm

The only drongo found on Aldabra Island. Ad. is a small bird with an unusually short and thick bill. Juv. very unlike ad., with a thinner bill, dark upperparts and mottled grey underparts. Active in pairs or family parties displaying typical drongo-like flycatching behaviour. Chases after Pied Crows. HABITAT Mangroves, and thickets of the larger trees. STATUS Uncommon endemic to Aldabra. CALL A chirruped 'chrit chrit che cha' phrase and softer 'chwit chwit' notes.

4 GRANDE COMORE DRONGO
Dicrurus fuscipennis ■ 24 cm

The only drongo found on Grande Comore. Typical drongo-like shape, stance and behaviour but has a shorter, less markedly forked tail than region's other drongos. Juv. similar to ad. but has a very slightly forked tail. HABITAT Forests, forest edge, degraded forest. STATUS Uncommon endemic to Grande Comore, found on slopes of Mt. Karthala, in particular the north-western ones. CALL Typical drongo squeaks and sharp clicks, and a softer 'wit wit' note.

5 PIED CROW
Corvus albus ■ 46–50 cm

The region's only large black and white crow. A conspicuous and bold bird, gathering sometimes in large flocks but usually in pairs or small groups. Often soars at great heights and readily rides thermals, appearing like a bird of prey. HABITAT Found in a wide variety of habitats, from beaches, grasslands and woodlands to environs of towns. Avoids dense forests. STATUS Common on Comoros, the Aldabras and Madagascar. CALL Typical crow-like 'caw caw' and throaty gurgles.

6 HOUSE CROW
Corvus splendens ■ 34–48 cm

This small, grey and black crow is unmistakeable and unlikely to be confused with much larger Pied Crow as it lacks any white coloration. Grey on body is variable but always contrasts with black head, wings and tail. Juv. duller version of ad. HABITAT Never far from human habitation. STATUS Colonized Mauritius and Seychelles, but may be extinct on the latter. CALL A high-pitched 'caw caw'.

1 MADAGASCAR FODY   *Foudia madagascariensis* ■ 14 cm
Unmistakeable: a small, brightly coloured, social bird with a black eye-stripe, dark-brown wings and tail, and a short, black, conical bill. In breeding plumage distinguished from male Forest Fody by its bright-red belly and undertail coverts, and bright-red, black-streaked mantle. Non-br. male, with its pale-coloured bill, olive-brown upperparts with brown streaks, and brownish-grey underparts, is very difficult to distinguish from Forest Fody, but general plumage hue is greyish brown and the bill is weaker. Distinguished from female House Sparrow (p. 170) by its smaller size, proportionally stronger conical bill and lighter greyish-brown upperparts. When acquiring breeding plumage, male may show a red head and breast and a greyish belly, coloration similar to that of the male Forest Fody in breeding plumage. Female and juv. similar to male in non-breeding plumage. HABITAT All strata of all types of original forest; secondary growth; gardens; wood plantations; cultivated land, man-made wooded savanna; from sea level to very high altitude. Observed in groups, sometimes very large ones, and often associated in the forest with mixed-species flocks. STATUS Endemic to Madagascar, found throughout the island, where very common. Introduced to and common on Réunion, Mauritius, Rodrigues, Seychelles and the four islands of Comoros. CALL A vocal species; utters a very high-pitched 'cheeet cheet cheet' trill from a high, unconcealed perch.

2 FOREST FODY   *Foudia omissa* ■ 14 cm
Small, plump, forest bird with red head, chest, and uppertail coverts; black eye-stripe; dark-brown wings, mantle, back, and tail; and short, black, conical bill. Distinguished from male Madagascar Fody in breeding plumage by its grey belly and undertail coverts, and brown mantle with black streaks. Non-br. male has light-brown bill, olive-brown upperparts with brown streaks, and brownish-grey underparts. Very difficult to distinguish from non-br. Madagascar Fody, but bill is stronger, and general plumage hue is greenish-brown. Female similar to male in non-breeding plumage; juv. similar to female. HABITAT All strata of rain forest and adjacent secondary growth, from sea level to high altitude. Observed in small groups and often associated with mixed-species flocks. STATUS Endemic to Madagascar; found in east, where uncommon. CALL A vocal species; utters a very high-pitched 'cheeet cheet cheet' trill similar to that of Madagascar Fody.

3 ALDABRA FODY   *Foudia aldabrana* ■ 13–15 cm
The only fody found on Aldabra and unlikely to be confused with any of the island's other small birds. Male in breeding plumage is very much brighter than other closely related fodies. It has a vivid red head and breast, the latter extending well onto lower breast to contrast with a bright-yellow belly. Some birds show an overall bright orangey-yellow plumage but they are thought to be rare and aberrant. The species is overall chunkier and bigger than other fodies, with a larger and thicker-based bill and larger black eye-mask. HABITAT Casuarina stands, mangroves, and other suitable woodland. STATUS Common endemic to Aldabra Island, Seychelles. CALL Similar to that of Madagascar Fody.

1 MAURITIUS FODY
Foudia rubra ■ 14 cm

The male in breeding plumage, with bright red-head and breast contrasting with olive belly, is unmistakeable. Female, juv. and non-br. male very difficult to distinguish from similar-plumaged Madagascar Fody (p. 166). The species differs from Madagascar Fody in its behaviour, regularly taking nectar from flowers and creeping woodpecker-like along branches looking for insects under the bark. Its bill is finer and longer than that of Madagascar Fody. HABITAT Natural forests, forest edge and adjoining heathland. STATUS Uncommon endemic to Mauritius. CALL Various 'chip chip' notes and harsher calls.

2 COMORO FODY
Foudia eminentissima ■ 12–14 cm

Breeding male differs from br. male Madagascar Fody (p. 166) in the extent of the red plumage, which is confined to the head and breast. Non-br. male, female and juv. all resemble Madagascar Fody of similar sex and age, and are very difficult to tell apart unless habitat preference and calls are noted. Generally, a fody seen deep inside natural forest would be the Comoro Fody. HABITAT Prefers natural forest but has adapted to secondary scrub, alien plantations and gardens. STATUS Locally common endemic to all four islands of the Comoros. CALL A buzzing 'weeeez' or 'shweeez' and a rapid 'kaa kaa kaa'.

3 RODRIGUES FODY
Foudia flavicans ■ 12–13 cm

The breeding male, with its bright orange-yellow face and breast, is unlikely to be confused with any other bird on Rodrigues. Non-br. male distinguished from non-br. male, female and juv. Madagascar Fody (p. 166) by the yellow wash over their faces. Nevertheless female and juv. difficult to tell from similar-plumaged Madagascar Fody except by behaviour and habitat. The Rodrigues Fody sometimes behaves like a tiny woodpecker, working its way along branches to inspect the bark for insects. HABITAT Remnant forest patches; exotic trees and shrubbery. STATUS Rare endemic to Rodrigues Island, Mascarenes. CALL A fast 'chip chip chip' and a deeper 'chuk chuk'.

4 SEYCHELLES FODY
Foudia sechellarum ■ 12–13 cm

Breeding male identified by the yellowish-orange wash across its face and by its black bill. Non-br. male, female and juv. resemble similar-plumaged Madagascar Fody (p. 166) but are larger and chunkier in build, and lack streaking on mantle and wings to produce a more uniform olive-brown coloration. HABITAT Open sandy clearings, low shrub and wooded coastal areas. STATUS Endemic to the central Seychelles, where it occurs on Cousin, Cousine and Frégate islands. CALL 'Tsk tsk' contact call, and a chattering alarm call.

1 HOUSE SPARROW
Passer domesticus ■ 13–14 cm

The male's chestnut mantle, grey crown and black bib are diagnostic of one of the world's best-known small birds. Madagascar Mannikin (p. 172) also has a black bib and brown back but is diminutive in size. Female and juv. House Sparrow are dowdy, nondescript grey and brown birds which resemble female fodies but lack the latters' streaking. HABITAT Never far from human habitation. STATUS Introduced into or has colonized many islands. CALL Familiar chirrups, chips and 'chissick' call notes.

2 SAKALAVA WEAVER
Ploceus sakalava ■ 15 cm

Has a bright-yellow head, throat, and upperbreast; greyish underparts and greyish-brown upperparts streaked with dark brown, and a bare reddish circle around the eye. Non-br. male has greyish-brown upperparts with brown streaks, greyish underparts, light-grey bill, and head marked by large, pale eyebrow. Distinguished from Madagascar Fody (p. 166) in non-br. plumage by larger size, stronger bill, paler general hue, and rosy circle around the eye. HABITAT Woodland, gallery forest, deciduous dry forest, subarid thorn scrub and secondary growth. Found in groups, especially near colonial breeding site. STATUS Endemic to Madagascar; common in north, west and south. CALL A high-pitched 'dji dji dji dji'.

3 NELICOURVI WEAVER
Ploceus nelicourvi ■ 15 cm

Small, stocky, black-headed forest bird with bright golden-yellow throat, upper breast and nape, rufous undertail coverts, grey belly, yellow-green upperparts and wings and brownish tail. Female differs from male in its pale-yellow head with greenish crown, the stripe across the eye and its generally duller plumage. Juv. differs from female in its greenish forehead. HABITAT Rain forest and adjacent secondary growth. Non-colonial; often associated with mixed-species flocks, especially with greenbuls. STATUS Endemic to Madagascar; commonly found in east and north. CALL Utters an unmelodious 'tiang tiang tiang'.

4 VILLAGE (SPOTTED-BACKED) WEAVER
Ploceus cucullatus ■ 14–16 cm

The breeding male, with its black face and spangled yellow and black back, is unmistakeable. Non-br. male and female are a dowdy brown and buff, and might be confused with similar-plumaged fodies but lack their streaking. HABITAT Farm- and scrublands, wooded areas. STATUS Introduced to Mauritius and Réunion; common. CALL A throaty 'chuck chuck'; swizzling notes when displaying.

5 CAPE CANARY
Serinus canicollis ■ 11–13 cm

Can be confused with Yellow-eyed Canary but has an obvious grey head and yellow face. Female slightly duller. Juv. is a dowdy olive bird, heavily streaked on the underparts. Occurs in small flocks at high altitudes. HABITAT Grassy areas and scrublands. STATUS Introduced to and common on Réunion at higher altitudes. CALL A trilling flight call and typical canary-like song.

6 YELLOW-EYED CANARY
Serinus mozambicus ■ 10–12 cm

The region's only small, greenish-yellow bird with a bright-yellow rump. Could be confused with Cape Canary but lacks the latter's grey head and yellow face. Differs from female Village Weaver in its much smaller size and its contrasting yellow (not uniform olive) rump. HABITAT Farm- and scrublands and lightly wooded areas. STATUS Introduced to the Mascarenes and Assumption Island, Seychelles. CALL A 'zeee-zeree-chereeo' and a buzzy canary song.

171

1 BRONZE MANNIKIN   *Spermestes cucullatus* ■ 9 cm
A tiny brown and white bird with a black face, blue and black bill, and barred flanks and rump. At close range the bird shows an obvious bronzy green shoulder patch. Juv. is a drab uniform brown with paler vent. HABITAT Old cultivated areas, grasslands and scrub, and gardens around villages. STATUS Probably introduced to Comoros; common on all four islands. CALL A soft, buzzy 'chizza chizza'.

2 SPICE FINCH   *Lonchura punctulata* ■ 11 cm
Small, brownish finch with brown bib and scaly breast and flanks, and grey bill and legs. Not likely to be confused with any of the region's other birds. HABITAT Farm- and scrublands and grassy areas. STATUS Introduced to Mauritius, Réunion, where it is common on the former and less common on the latter. CALL A short 'ki-dee'.

3 RED AVADAVAT   *Amandava amandava* ■ 10 cm
A tiny red and brown bird with white spotting on its back and on sides of breast and flanks. The bright red rump is noticeable in flight. Female and non-br. male have less red, and show white spotting only on wings. HABITAT Long-grassed areas; wetland fringes. STATUS Introduced to Mascarenes, where uncommon on Réunion; extinct on Mauritius. Not found on Rodrigues. CALL A high-pitched 'pseep'.

4 MADAGASCAR MANNIKIN   *Lonchura nana* ■ 9 cm
Very small, gregarious passerine with short, conical, greyish-pink bill, brown top to head, grey-brown cheeks, black bib and lores. Rest of plumage shows tan underparts with finely striped undertail coverts, and dark grey-brown upperparts except for finely striped uppertail coverts and dark-brown tail. Distinguished from Common Waxbill by smaller size, shorter tail, black bill, light-brown breast and belly and black bib. Juv. differs from ad. in its overall brown plumage, absence of black bib, and entirely dark bill. HABITAT Open habitats, including forest edges and clearings in all natural forest types, secondary growth, gardens, cultivated areas, man-made wooded savanna; from sea level to very high altitude. Observed in groups. STATUS Endemic to Madagascar; very common throughout island. CALL A fairly quiet species, uttering a succession of thin, harmonious 'tsee tsee' notes in flight.

5 JAVA SPARROW   *Padda oryzivora* ■ 16 cm
Easily identified by its grey body, black head and white cheeks. Juv. is a dowdier version of ad. HABITAT Farm- and scrublands, grassy areas, and close to human habitation. STATUS Introduced to Mascarenes; has survived only on Mauritius. CALL A 'tup tup' flight note.

6 COMMON WAXBILL   *Estrilda astrild* ■ 11–12 cm
A tiny brown bird with a long pointed tail; when seen close to, reveals very fine barring on upper- and underparts. Also has a lozenge-shaped red patch around the eye and red central belly and vent. Unlikely to be confused with any of the region's other small birds. HABITAT Long grass, thickets and reed beds. STATUS Introduced to the Mascarenes and Seychelles groups; recently found in the north-west part of Madagascar. Gregarious. CALL A nasal 'cher cher cher', and a 'ping ping' flight note.

1

juv.

ad.

2

3

♀

♂

4

5

6

VAGRANTS TO THE REGION

The following species have been recorded fewer than ten times in the region:

Rockhopper Penguin	*Eudyptes chrysocome*	Long-toed Stint	*Calidris subminuta*
Wandering Albatross	*Diomedea exulans*	Pectoral Sandpiper	*Calidris melanotus*
Dark-mantled Sooty		Sharp-tailed Sandpiper	*Calidris acuminata*
Albatross	*Phoebetria fusca*	Buff-breasted Sandpiper	*Tryngites subruficollis*
Light-mantled Sooty		Broad-billed Sandpiper	*Caldiris falcinellus*
Albatross	*Phoebetria palpebrata*	Common Snipe	*Gallinago gallinago*
Northern Giant Petrel	*Macronectes halli*	Pintail Snipe	*Gallinago stenura*
Slender-billed Prion	*Pachyptila belcheri*	Great Snipe	*Gallinago media*
Broad-billed Prion	*Pachyptila vittata*	Little Curlew	*Numenius minutus*
Fairy Prion	*Pachyptila turtur*	Redshank	*Tringa totanus*
Swinhoe's Storm Petrel	*Oceanodrama monorhis*	Green Sandpiper	*Tringa ochropus*
Red-billed Tropicbird	*Phaethon aethereus*	Grey-tailed Tatler	*Heteroscelus brevipes*
Great Cormorant	*Phalacrocorax carbo*	Red-necked Phalarope	*Phalaropus lobatus*
Goliath Heron	*Ardea goliath*	Black Tern	*Chlidonias niger*
Black-headed Heron	*Ardea melanocephala*	European Turtle Dove	*Streptopelia turtur*
Indian Pond Heron	*Ardeola grayii*	Jacobin Cuckoo	*Oxylophus jacobinus*
Intermediate Egret	*Egretta intermedia*	Great-spotted Cuckoo	*Clamator glandarius*
Great Bittern	*Botaurus stellaris*	Common Cuckoo	*Cuculus canorus*
Cinnamon Bittern	*Ixobrychus cinnamoneus*	Asian Lesser Cuckoo	*Cuculus poliocephalus*
Sacred Ibis	*Threskiornis aethiopicus*	Brown Fish Owl	*Ketupa zeylonensis*
White Stork	*Ciconia ciconia*	European Scops Owl	*Otus scops*
Ruddy Shelduck	*Tadorna ferruginea*	European Nightjar	*Caprimulgus europaeus*
Northern Pintail	*Anas acuta*	White-throated Needletail	*Hirundapus caudacutus*
Northern Shoveler	*Anas clypeata*	Pacific Swift	*Apus pacificus*
Long-crested Eagle	*Lophaetus occipitalis*	Greater Short-toed Lark	*Calandrella brachydactyla*
Osprey	*Pandion haliaetus*	House Martin	*Delichon urbica*
Booted Eagle	*Hieraaetus pennatus*	Lesser Striped Swallow	*Hirundo abyssinica*
European Marsh Harrier	*Circus aeruginosus*	Grey Wagtail	*Motacilla cinerea*
Black-shouldered Kite	*Elanus caeruleus*	Common Redstart	*Phoenicurus phoenicurus*
Lesser Kestrel	*Falco naumanni*	Whinchat	*Saxicola rubetra*
Western Red-footed Falcon	*Falco vespertinus*	Isabelline Wheatear	*Oenanthe isabellina*
European Hobby	*Falco subbuteo*	European Rock-Thrush	*Monticola saxatilis*
Corncrake	*Crex crex*	European Sedge Warbler	*Acrocephalus schoenobaenus*
Spotted Crake	*Porzana porzana*	Icterine Warbler	*Hippolais icterina*
Striped Crake	*Porzana marginalis*	Willow Warbler	*Phylloscopus trochilus*
White-breasted Waterhen	*Amaurornis phoenicurus*	Wood Warbler	*Phylloscopus sibilatrix*
Watercock	*Gallicrex cinerea*	Common Whitethroat	*Sylvia communis*
European Oystercatcher	*Haematopus ostralegus*	Blackcap	*Sylvia atricapilla*
Red-winged (Collared)		European Golden Oriole	*Oriolus oriolus*
Pratincole	*Glareola pratincola*	Red-backed Shrike	*Lanius collurio*
Oriental Pratincole	*Glareola maldivarus*	Lesser Grey Shrike	*Lanius minor*
Black-winged Pratincole	*Glareola nordmanni*	Woodchat Shrike	*Lanius senator*
Oriental Plover	*Charadrius veredus*	Rose-coloured Starling	*Sturnus roseus*
Pied (Eurasian) Avocet	*Recurvirostra avosetta*	Wattled Starling	*Creatophora cinerea*
Great Knot	*Calidris tenuirostris*	Common Rosefinch	*Carpodacus erythrinus*
Temminck's Stint	*Calidris temminckii*	Ortolan Bunting	*Emberiza hortulana*

Glossary of Terms

Accidental A vagrant or stray species not normally found within the region.

Arboreal Tree-dwelling.

Breeding endemic A species which breeds in one particular area and migrates to another.

Colonial Associating in close proximity while roosting, feeding or nesting.

Coverts Groups of feathers covering specific parts of the bird (the bases of the major flight-feathers, for instance, or the ears).

Crepuscular Active at dawn and dusk.

Crest Raised feathers of the crown, forehead or nape.

Cryptic Pertaining to camouflage coloration.

Carpal The bend of the wing at carpal joint.

Cere Bare skin at base of bill on birds of prey.

Decurved Downward curving.

Diagnostic Pertaining to a feature or character which is especially useful in identifying a species.

Dimorphic Includes sexual dimorphism where male and female are different or exist in two distinct colour forms.

Diurnal Active during daylight hours.

Eclipse plumage Drab plumage which occurs in some male ducks and sunbirds during a transitional moult after breeding.

Endemic A species whose sole distribution is restricted to one particular area.

Eyebrow A stripe above the eye.

Facial disc A bird's face that is disc-like in form, well-defined and typically flat in owls.

Feral Species that have escaped from captivity and maintain viable populations in the wild.

Flight feathers The longest wing and tail feathers.

Flush Put to flight.

Form A colour variation within a species.

Fulvous Creamy brown, reddish-yellow or tawny coloration.

Immature All stages of plumage except adult (includes juvenile).

Juvenile The distinctive first, full-feathered plumage of a young bird.

Leading edge The front edge of a wing.

Mantle The combined area of the back, upperwings and scapulars.

Mask A dark mark on the head usually covering the forehead, eyes and ear coverts.

Migrant A species that undertakes (usually) long-distance flights between its breeding and non-breeding areas.

Montane Pertaining to mountains.

Moustache A stripe running from the base of the bill down the side of the throat.

Nocturnal Active at night.

Pelagic Frequenting the open oceans, well away from land.

Phase A stage in plumage coloration.

Race A term used for a subspecies within a specific geographical area.

Range A bird's distribution.

Raptor Diurnal bird of prey.

Resident A non-migratory species which remains in the same area all year.

Scapulars The groups of feathers, on the upperparts, at the base of the upperwing.

Secondaries The longest wing feathers on the back (extending from mid-wing to wing-base).

Soaring Flight sustained by upward moving air with little movement of wings.

Speculum A distinctive patch of colour on the secondaries of ducks.

Subspecies A bird population which can be distinguished from other members of the same species.

Terrestrial Ground-dwelling.

Territory The established area a bird defends for breeding and feeding.

Trailing edge The hind edge of the wing.

Vent The area which covers the lower belly to undertail feathers.

Vagrant Rare and accidental to the region.

ILLUSTRATED GLOSSARY

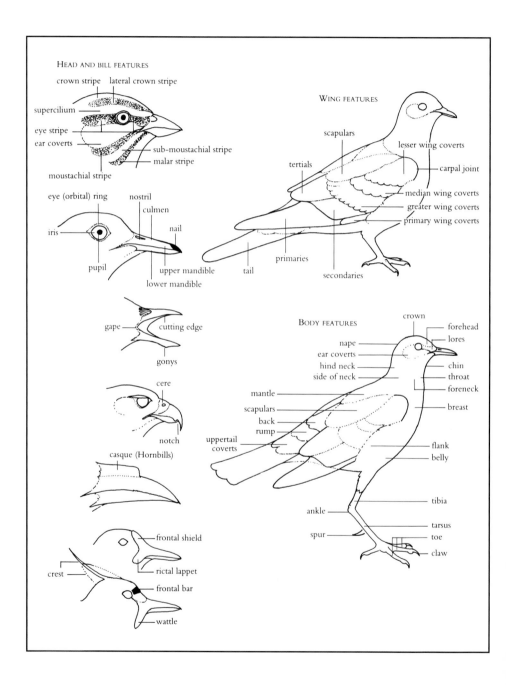

HEAD AND BILL FEATURES

crown stripe   lateral crown stripe

supercilium

eye stripe

ear coverts

sub-moustachial stripe

malar stripe

moustachial stripe

eye (orbital) ring   nostril

culmen

iris   nail

pupil   upper mandible   tail

lower mandible

gape   cutting edge

gonys

cere

notch

casque (Hornbills)

frontal shield

crest

rictal lappet

frontal bar

wattle

WING FEATURES

scapulars

lesser wing coverts

carpal joint

tertials

median wing coverts

greater wing coverts

primary wing coverts

primaries

secondaries

BODY FEATURES   crown

forehead

lores

nape

ear coverts

hind neck

side of neck

chin

throat

foreneck

mantle

scapulars

breast

back

rump

uppertail coverts

flank

belly

tibia

ankle

tarsus

spur

toe

claw

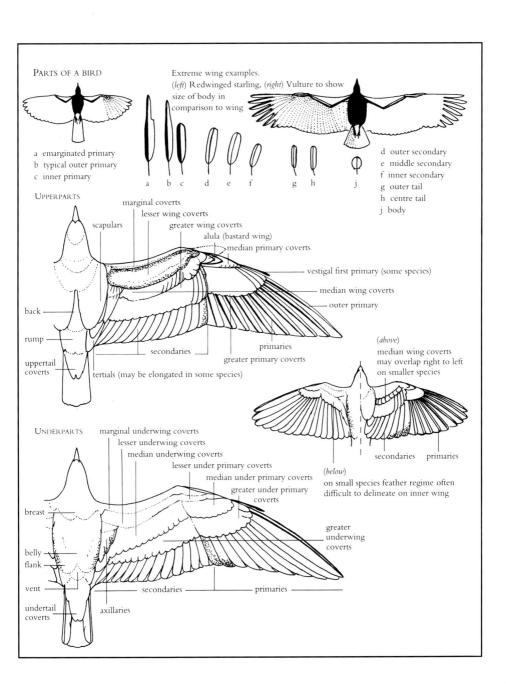

PARTS OF A BIRD

Extreme wing examples.
(*left*) Redwinged starling, (*right*) Vulture to show size of body in comparison to wing

a emarginated primary
b typical outer primary
c inner primary

a b c d e f g h j

d outer secondary
e middle secondary
f inner secondary
g outer tail
h centre tail
j body

UPPERPARTS

marginal coverts
lesser wing coverts
scapulars
greater wing coverts
alula (bastard wing)
median primary coverts

vestigal first primary (some species)

median wing coverts

outer primary

back

rump

uppertail coverts

secondaries
tertials (may be elongated in some species)
greater primary coverts
primaries

(*above*)
median wing coverts may overlap right to left on smaller species

secondaries primaries

UNDERPARTS

marginal underwing coverts
lesser underwing coverts
median underwing coverts
lesser under primary coverts
median under primary coverts
greater under primary coverts

(*below*)
on small species feather regime often difficult to delineate on inner wing

breast

greater underwing coverts

belly
flank

vent

secondaries primaries

undertail coverts
axillaries

BIBLIOGRAPHY

Amin, A., Willets, D & Skerrett, A. 1995. *Aldabra, World Heritage Site*. Camerapix; Kenya.

Barré, N. & Barau, A. 1982. *Oiseaux de la Réunion*. Imprimerie des Arts Graphiques Modernes; Saint-Denis.

Berlioz, J. 1946. *Oiseaux de la Réunion*. Faune de l'Empire Français; Vol. IV. Librairie Larose; Paris.

Collar, N. J. & Stuart, S. N. 1985. *Threatened Birds of Africa and Related Islands*. The ICBP/IUCN Red Data Book; Part 1. International Council for Bird Preservation; Cambridge.

Diamond, A. W. 1987. *Studies of Mascarene Island Birds*. Cambridge University Press; Cambridge.

Dee, T. J. 1986. *The Endemic Birds of Madagascar*. International Council for Bird Preservation; Cambridge.

Dowsett, R. J. & Forbes-Watson, A. D. 1993. *Checklist of Birds of the Afrotropical and Malagasy Regions*. Tauraco Press; Liège.

Gardner, N. 1992. *A Birder's Guide to Travel in Madagascar*. Privately published.

Langrand, O. 1990. *Guide to the Birds of Madagascar*. Yale University Press; New Haven & London.

Langrand, O. 1995. *Guide des Oiseaux de Madagascar*. Delachaux & Niestlé; Lausanne.

Louette, M. 1988. *Les Oiseaux des Comores*. Musée Royal de l'Afrique Centrale; Tervuren.

Michel, C. 1992. *Birds of Mauritius*. Rosehill; Mauritius.

Milne-Edwards, A. & Grandidier, A. 1878–1885. *Histoire Naturelle des Oiseaux*. In *Histoire Physique, Politique, et Naturelle de Madagascar*. Imprimerie Nationale; Paris.

Milon, P., Petter, J-J. & Randrianasolo, G. 1973. *Oiseaux*, 2 vols. Faune de Madagascar Vol. XXXV; Tananarive & Paris.

Penny, M. 1974. *The Birds of Seychelles and Outlying Islands*. Collins; London.

Seaton, A.J., Beaver, K. & Afif, M. 1991. *A Focus on Aldabra; Conserving the Environment*. Ministry of Education; Victoria.

Sinclair, I., Hockey, P., & Tarboton, W. 1997. *Sasol Guide to Birds of Southern Africa*. 2nd ed. Struik; Cape Town.

Skerrett, A. & Bullock, I. 1992. *A Birdwatcher's Guide to the Seychelles*. Prion; Seychelles.

Staub, F. 1976. *Birds of the Mascarenes and Saint-Brandon*. Organisation Normale des Entreprises LTEE; Port Louis.

Thibault, J-C. & Guyot, I. 1988. *Livre Rouge des Oiseaux Menacés des Régions Françaises d'Outre-mer*. International Council for Bird Preservation; Saint-Cloud.

Wheatley, N. 1995. *Where to Watch Birds in Africa*. Helm; London.

USEFUL ADDRESSES

MADAGASCAR

Association Nationale pour la Gestion des Aires Protegées (ANGAP) (National Association for Management of Protected Areas), BP 1424 Antananarivo (101) Madagascar.
Tel: (261) 20 22 305 18; fax: (261) 20 22 319 94

Direction des Eaux et Forêts (Directorate of Water and Forests), BP 243 Antananarivo (101) Madagascar.
Tel: (261) 20 22 406 10

Working Group on Birds in the Madagascar Region, c/o Steven M. Goodman, WWF, BP 738 Antananarivo (101) Madagascar.
Tel: (261) 20 22 346 38; fax: (261) 20 22 348 88

RÉUNION

Société d'Etudes Ornithologiques de la Réunion, Musée d'Histoire Naturelle, Rue Poivre, 97400 Saint-Denis, Réunion-France.
Tel: (262) 20 02 19; fax: (262) 21 33 93.

MAURITIUS

Mauritius Wildlife Appeal Fund (MWAF), Tamarin, Mauritius.

SEYCHELLES

Nature Protection Trust of Seychelles, P.O. Box 207, Mahé, Seychelles.

Seychelles Bird Records Committee, c/o Adrian Skerrett, P.O. Box 336, Mahé, Seychelles.

INDEX TO SCIENTIFIC NAMES

Accipiter francesiae 64
A. henstii 60
A. madagascariensis 64
Acridotheres tristis 162
Acrocephalus newtoni 142
A. rodericanus 144
A. sechellensis 144
Actitis hypoleucos 84
Actophilornis albinucha 76
Agapornis cana 104
Alectroenas madagascariensis 100
A. pulcherrima 100
A. sganzini 100
Amandava amandava 172
Amaurornis olivieri 74
Amphilais seebohmi 142
Anas bernieri 56
A. erythrorhyncha 56
A. hottentota 56
A. melleri 56
A. querquedula 56
Anastomus lamelligerus 54
Anhinga rufa 44
Anous stolidus 96
A. tenuirostris 96
Anthus cervinus 136
A. trivialis 136
Apus affinis 116
A. apus 116
A. balstoni 116
A. melba 116
Ardea cinerea 50
A. humbloti 50
A. purpurea 50
Ardeola idae 46
A. ralloides 46
Arenaria interpres 76
Asio capensis 112
A. madagascariensis 112
Atelornis crossleyi 124
A. pittoides 124
Aviceda madagascariensis 62
Aythya innotata 58
Bernieria apperti 130
B. cinereiceps 130
B. madagascariensis 130
B. tenebrosa 130
B. zosterops 130
Brachypteracias leptosomus 124

B. squamiger 124
Bubulcus ibis 48
Bulweria fallax 38
Buteo brachypterus 62
Butorides striatus 46
Calicalicus madagascariensis 158
C. rufocarpalis 158
Calidris alba 86
C. ferruginea 86
C. minuta 86
Calonectris diomedea 38
Canirallus kioloides 70
Caprimulgus enarratus 114
C. madagascariensis 114
Casmerodius albus 48
Catharacta antarctica 88
Centropus toulou 106
Charadrius asiaticus 86
C. dubius 80
C. hiaticula 80
C. leschenaultii 86
C. marginatus 80
C. mongolus 86
C. pecuarius 80
C. thoracicus 80
C. tricollaris 80
Chlidonias hybridus 92
C. leucopterus 92
Circus maillardi 62
Cisticola cherina 140
Collocalia elaphra 118
C. francica 118
Columba livia 98
C. polleni 102
Copsychus albospecularis 132
C. sechellarum 132
Coracias garrulus 122
Coracina cinerea 162
C. cucullata 162
C. newtoni 162
C. typica 162
Coracopsis barklyi 104
C. nigra 104
C. vasa 104
Corvus albus 164
C. splendens 164
Corythornis vintsioides 120
Coturnix chinensis 68
C. coturnix 68
C. delegorguei 68

Coua caerulea 110
C. coquereli 108
C. cristata 110
C. cursor 108
C. gigas 108
C. olivaceiceps 108
C. reynaudii 110
C. ruficeps 108
C. serriana 110
C. verreauxi 110
Crossleyia xanthophrys 130
Cryptosylvicola randrianasoloi 146
Cuculus rochii 106
Cyanolanius comorensis 156
C. madagascarinus 156
Cypsiurus parvus 116
Daption capense 36
Dendrocygna bicolor 58
D. viduata 58
Dicrurus aldabranus 164
D. forficatus 164
D. fuscipennis 164
D. waldenii 164
Diomedea cauta 34
D. chlororynchos 34
D. melanophris 34
Dromaeocercus brunneus 142
Dromas ardeola 78
Dryolimnas aldabranus 72
D. cuvieri 72
Egretta ardesiaca 48
E. dimorpha 48
Estrilda astrild 172
Euryceros prevostii 158
Eurystomus glaucurus 122
Eutriorchis astur 60
Falco araea 66
F. concolor 66
F. eleonorae 66
F. newtoni 66
F. peregrinus 64
F. punctatus 66
F. zoniventris 64
Falculea palliata 158
Foudia aldabrana 166
F. eminentissima 168
F. flavicans 168
F. madagascariensis 166
F. omissa 166
F. rubra 168

F. sechellarum 168
Francolinus pondicerianus 68
Fregata ariel 42
F. minor 42
Fregetta grallaria 40
F. tropica 40
Fulica cristata 74
Gallinago macrodactyla 76
Gallinula chloropus 74
Gelochelidon nilotica 94
Geopelia striata 98
Glareola ocularis 76
Gygis alba 96
Haliaeetus vociferoides 60
Hartertula flavoviridis 146
Hartlaubius auratus 162
Himantopus himantopus 78
Hirundo rustica 118
Humblotia flavirostris 138
Hydroprogne caspia 90
Hypositta corallirostris 156
Hypsipetes borbonicus 128
  H. crassirostris 128
  H. madagascariensis 128
  H. olivaceus 128
  H. parvirostris 128
Ispidina madagascariensis 120
Ixobrychus minutus 46
  I. sinensis 46
Larus cirrocephalus 90
  L. dominicanus 90
  L. fuscus 90
  L. ridibundus 90
Leptopterus chabert 156
  L. viridis 156
Leptosomus discolor 122
  L. gracilis 122
Limosa lapponica 82
  L. limosa 82
Lonchura nana 172
  L. punctulata 172
Lophotibis cristata 52
Macheiramphus alcinus 64
Macronectes giganteus 34
Margaroperdix madagascariensis 68
Merops persicus 120
  M. superciliosus 120
Mesitornis unicolor 70
  M. variegata 70
Milvus aegyptius 62
  M. migrans 62
Mirafra hova 140
Monias benschi 70

Monticola erythronotus 134
  M. imerinus 134
  M. sharpei 134
Motacilla alba 136
  M. flava 136
  M. flaviventris 136
Musicapa striata 138
Mycteria ibis 54
Mystacornis crossleyi 132
Nectarinia abbotti 154
  N. comorensis 154
  N. coquerellii 154
  N. dussumieri 152
  N. humbloti 152
  N. moebii 152
  N. notata 152
  N. souimanga 154
Neodrepanis coruscans 126
  N. hypoxantha 126
Neomixis striatigula 146
  N. tenella 146
  N. viridis 146
Nesillas aldabrana 144
  N. brevicaudata 144
  N. lantzii 142
  N. mariae 144
  N. typica 142
Nesoenas mayeri 102
Nettapus auritus 58
Newtonia amphichroa 140
  N. archboldi 140
  N. brunneicauda 140
  N. fanovanae 140
Ninox superciliaris 112
Numenius arquata 82
  N. phaeopus 82
Numida meleagris 68
Nycticorax nycticorax 46
Oceanites oceanicus 40
Oena capensis 100
Oenanthe oenanthe 134
Oriolia bernieri 158
Otus capnodes 114
  O. insularis 114
  O. pauliani 114
  O. rutilus 114
Oxylabes madagascariensis 132
Pachycoccyx audeberti 106
Padda oryzivora 172
Passer domesticus 170
Pelagodroma marina 40
Pelecanus rufescens 44
Phaethon lepturus 42
  P. rubricauda 42

Phalacrocorax africanus 44
Phedina borbonica 118
Philepitta castanea 126
  P. schlegeli 126
Philomachus pugnax 76
Phoenicopterus minor 54
  P. ruber 54
Platalea alba 52
Plegadis falcinellus 52
Ploceus cucullatus 170
  P. nelicourvi 170
  P. sakalava 170
Pluvialis fulva 78
  P. squatarola 78
Polyboroides radiatus 60
Porphyrio porphyrio 74
Porphyrula alleni 74
Porzana pusilla 74
Pseudobias wardi 138
Psittacula echo 104
  P. krameri 104
Pterocles personatus 98
Pterodroma arminjoniana 36
  P. aterrima 38
  P. baraui 36
  P. macroptera 38
  P. mollis 36
Puffinus atrodorsalis 36
  P. carneipes 38
  P. lherminieri 36
  P. pacificus 38
Pycnonotus jocosus 128
Rallus madagascariensis 72
Randia pseudozosterops 146
Riparia paludicola 118
  R. riparia 118
Rostratula benghalensis 76
Sarkidiornis melanotos 58
Sarothrura insularis 72
  S. watersi 72
Saxicola tectes 134
  S. torquata 134
Schetba rufa 158
Scopus umbretta 52
Serinus canicollis 170
  S. mozambicus 170
Spermestes cucullatus 172
Stercorarius longicaudus 88
  S. parasiticus 88
  S. pomarinus 88
Sterna albifrons/saundersi 96
  S. anaethetus 96
  S. bengalensis 94
  S. bergii 94

S. *dougallii* 92
S. *fuscata* 96
S. *hirundo* 92
S. *sandvicensis* 94
S. *sumatrana* 94
Streptopelia capicola 98
S. *chinensis* 98
S. *picturata* 102
S. *picturata coppingeri* 102
S. *picturata rostrata* 102
Sula dactylatra 44
S. *leucogaster* 44
S. *sula* 44
Tachybaptus pelzelnii 32
T. *ruficollis* 32
T. *rufolavatus* 32
Terpsiphone bourbonnensis 138

T. *corvina* 138
T. *mutata* 138
Thalassornis leuconotus 58
Thamnornis chloropetoides 142
Threskiornis bernieri 52
Treron australis 102
T. *griveaudi* 102
Tringa glareola 84
T. *nebularia* 82
T. *stagnatilis* 84
Turdus bewsheri 132
Turnix nigricollis 70
Turtur tympanistria 100
Tylas eduardi 160
Tyto alba 112
T. *soumagnei* 112
Upupa marginata 132

Uratelornis chimaera 124
Vanga curvirostris 160
Xenopirostris damii 160
X. *polleni* 160
X. *xenopirostris* 160
Xenus cinereus 84
Zoonavena grandidieri 116
Zosterops borbonicus 150
Z. *chloronothus* 150
Z. *kirki* 148
Z. *maderaspatanus* 148
Z. *mauritianus* 150
Z. *mayottensis* 148
Z. *modestus* 150
Z. *mouroniensis* 148
Z. *olivaceus* 150

INDEX TO ENGLISH COMMON NAMES

Albatross
Black-browed 34
Shy 34
Yellow-nosed 34
Asity
Schlegel's 126
Velvet 126
Avadavat, Red 172
Babbler, Crossley's 132
Bee-eater
Blue-cheeked 120
Madagascar 120
Bittern
Chinese *see* Bittern, Yellow
Little 46
Yellow 46
Booby
Brown 44
Masked 44
Red-footed 44
Bulbul
Comoro 128
Madagascar 128
Mauritius 128
Red-whiskered 128
Réunion 128
Seychelles 128
Button-Quail, Madagascar 70
Buzzard, Madagascar 62
Canary
Cape 170
Yellow-eyed 170
Cisticola, Madagascar 140
Coot, Red-knobbed 74
Cormorant, Reed 44
Coua
Blue 110
Coquerel's 108
Crested 110
Giant 108
Green-capped 108
Red-breasted 110
Red-capped 108
Red-fronted 110
Running 108
Verreaux's 110
Coucal, Madagascar 106
Crake, Baillon's 74
Crow
House 164
Pied 164

Cuckoo
Madagascar Lesser 106
Thick-billed 106
Cuckoo-Roller
Comoro 122
Madagascar 122
Cuckoo Shrike
Comoro 162
Madagascar 162
Mauritius 162
Réunion 162
Curlew, Eurasian 82
Dabchick 32
Darter, African 44
Dove
Barred Ground *see* Dove,
Zebra
Cape Turtle 98
Ground *see* Dove, Spotted
Madagascar Turtle 102
Namaqua 100
Seychelles Turtle 102
Spotted 98
Tambourine 100
Zebra 98
Drongo
Aldabra 164
Crested 164
Grande Comore 164
Mayotte 164
Duck
Fulvous 58
Knob-billed 58
Meller's 56
White-backed 58
White-faced 58
Eagle
Madagascar Fish 60
Madagascar Serpent 60
Egret
Black 48
Cattle 48
Dimorphic 48
Great White 48
Emutail
Brown 142
Grey 142
Falcon
Eleonora's 66
Peregrine 64
Sooty 66

Finch, Spice 172
Flamingo
Greater 54
Lesser 54
Flufftail
Madagascar 72
Slender-billed 72
Flycatcher
Humblot's 138
Madagascar Paradise 138
Mascarene Paradise 138
Seychelles Black Paradise
138
Spotted 138
Ward's 138
Fody
Aldabra 166
Comoro 168
Forest 166
Madagascar 166
Mauritius 168
Rodrigues 168
Seychelles 168
Francolin, Grey 68
Frigatebird
Greater 42
Lesser 42
Gallinule
Lesser 74
Purple 74
Garganey 56
Godwit
Bar-tailed 82
Black-tailed 82
Goose, Pygmy 58
Goshawk, Henst's 60
Grebe
Alaotra Little 32
Little 32
Madagascar Little 32
Greenbul
Appert's 130
Dusky 130
Grey-crowned 130
Long-billed 130
Spectacled 130
Greenshank, Common 82
Ground-Roller
Long-tailed 124
Pitta-like 124
Rufous-headed 124

Scaly 124
Short-legged 124
Guineafowl, Helmeted 68
Gull
  Black-headed 90
  Grey-headed 90
  Kelp 90
  Lesser Black-backed 90
Hamerkop 52
Harrier, Réunion 62
Hawk
  Bat 64
  Madagascar Cuckoo 62
  Madagascar Harrier 60
Heron
  Black-crowned Night 46
  Common Squacco 46
  Green-backed   46
  Grey 50
  Humblot's 50
  Madagascar Squacco 46
  Purple 50
  Striated *see* Heron,
    Greenbacked
Hoopoe, Madagascar 132
Ibis
  Glossy 52
  Madagascar Crested 52
  Madagascar Sacred 52
Jacana, Madagascar 76
Jery
  Common 146
  Green 146
  Stripe-throated 146
  Wedge-tailed 146
Kestrel
  Banded 64
  Madagascar 66
  Mauritius 66
  Seychelles 66
Kingfisher
  Madagascar 120
  Madagascar Pygmy 120
Kite
  Black 62
  Yellow-billed 62
Lark, Madagascar 140
Lovebird, Grey-headed 104
Magpie Robin
  Madagascar 132
  Seychelles 132
Mannikin
  Bronze 172
  Madagascar 172

Martin
  Brown-throated Sand 118
  Mascarene 118
  Sand 118
Mesite
  Brown 70
  Subdesert 70
  White-breasted 70
Moorhen, Common 74
Mynah, Common 162
Newtonia
  Archbold's 140
  Common 140
  Dark 140
  Red-tailed 140
Nightjar
  Collared 114
  Madagascar 114
Noddy
  Brown *see* Noddy, Common
  Common 96
  Lesser 96
Owl
  African Marsh 112
  Anjouan Scops 114
  Barn 112
  Karthala Scops 114
  Madagascar Long-eared 112
  Madagascar Red 112
  Madagascar Scops 114
  Seychelles Scops 114
  White-browed 112
Oxylabes
  White-throated 132
  Yellow-browed 130
Parakeet
  Echo *see* Parakeet, Mauritius
  Mauritius 104
  Ring-necked 104
Parrot
  Greater Vasa 104
  Lesser Vasa 104
  Seychelles Black 104
Partridge, Madagascar 68
Pelican, Pink-backed 44
Petrel
  Barau's 36
  Black-bellied Storm 40
  Great-winged 38
  Jouanin's 38
  Pintado 36
  Réunion 38
  Round Island *see* Petrel,
    Trinidade

Soft-plumaged 36
Southern Giant 34
Trinidade 36
White-bellied Storm 40
White-faced Storm 40
Wilson's Storm 40
Pigeon
  Comoro Blue 100
  Comoro Green 102
  Comoro Olive 102
  Feral 98
  Madagascar Blue 100
  Madagascar Green 102
  Pink 102
  Seychelles Blue 100
Pipit
  Red-throated 136
  Tree 136
Plover
  Caspian 86
  Common Ringed 80
  Crab 78
  Grey 78
  Kittlitz's 80
  Little Ringed 80
  Madagascar 80
  Pacific Golden 78
  Three-banded 80
  White-fronted 80
Pochard, Madagascar 58
Pratincole, Madagascar 76
Quail
  Blue-breasted 68
  Common 68
  Harlequin 68
Rail
  Aldabra 72
  Madagascar 72
  Madagascar Wood 70
  Sakalava 74
  White-throated 72
Robin, Magpie, *see* **Magpie**
  Robin
Rock-Thrush
  Amber Mountain 134
  Forest 134
  Littoral 134
Roller
  Broad-billed 122
  European 122
Ruff 76
Sanderling 86
Sandgrouse, Madagascar
  98

Sandpiper
  Common 84
  Curlew 86
  Marsh 84
  Terek 84
  Wood 84
Sandplover
  Greater 86
  Lesser 86
Shearwater
  Audubon's 36
  Cory's 38
  Flesh-footed 38
  Mascarene 36
  Wedge-tailed 38
Shrike, Cuckoo *see* **Cuckoo Shrike**
Skua
  Arctic 88
  Long-tailed 88
  Pomarine 88
  Subantarctic 88
Snipe
  Greater Painted 76
  Madagascar 76
Sparrow
  House 170
  Java 172
Sparrowhawk
  Frances's 64
  Madagascar 64
Spoonbill, African 52
Starling, Madagascar 162
Stilt, Black-winged 78
Stint, Little 86
Stonechat
  Common 134
  Réunion 134
Stork
  African Openbill 54
  Yellow-billed 54
Sunbird
  Abbott's 154
  Anjouan 154
  Comoro Green 152
  Humblot's 152
  Madagascar Green 152
  Mayotte 154
  Seychelles 152
  Souimanga 154

Sunbird-Asity
  Common 126
  Yellow-bellied 126
Swallow
  Barn 118
  European *see* Swallow, Barn
Swift
  African Palm 116
  Alpine 116
  Eurasian *see* Swift, European
  European 116
  Little 116
  Madagascar Black 116
  Madagascar Spine-tailed 116
Swiftlet
  Mascarene 118
  Seychelles 118
Teal
  Bernier's 56
  Hottentot 56
  Red-billed 56
Tern
  Black-naped 94
  Bridled 96
  Caspian 90
  Common 92
  Fairy *see* Tern, White
  Greater Crested *see* Tern, Swift
  Gull-billed 94
  Lesser Crested 94
  Little/Saunders' 96
  Roseate 92
  Sandwich 94
  Sooty 96
  Swift 94
  Whiskered 92
  White 96
  White-winged 92
Thrush, Comoro 132
Tropicbird
  Red-tailed 42
  White-tailed 42
Turnstone, Ruddy 76
Tylas 160
Vanga
  Bernier's 158
  Chabert's 156
  Comoro Blue 156
  Helmet 158

  Hook-billed 160
  Lafresnaye's 160
  Madagascar Blue 156
  Nuthatch 156
  Pollen's 160
  Red-shouldered 158
  Red-tailed 158
  Rufous 158
  Sickle-billed 158
  Van Dam's 160
  White-headed 156
Wagtail
  Madagascar 136
  White 136
  Yellow 136
Warbler
  Aldabra Brush 144
  Benson's Brush 144
  Comoro Brush 144
  Cryptic 146
  Madagascar Brush 142
  Madagascar Swamp 142
  Rand's 146
  Rodrigues 144
  Seychelles 144
  Subdesert Brush 142
  Thamnornis 142
Waxbill, Common 172
Weaver
  Nelicourvi 170
  Sakalava 170
  Spotted-backed *see* Weaver, Village
  Village 170
Wheatear
  European *see* Wheatear, Northern
  Northern 134
Whimbrel 82
White-eye
  Karthala 148
  Kirk's 148
  Madagascar 148
  Mauritius Grey 150
  Mauritius Olive 150
  Mayotte 148
  Réunion Grey 150
  Réunion Olive 150
  Seychelles 150